J

OVERNIGHT CAREER CHOICE

discover your ideal job in just a few hours

Second Edition

LAURENCE SHATKIN, Ph.D., and MICHAEL FARR

Also in JIST's Help in a Hurry Series

15-Minute Cover Letter

30-Day Job Promotion

30-Minute Resume Makeover

Next-Day Job Interview

Next-Day Salary Negotiation

One-Hour College Application Essay

Same-Day Resume

Today's Hot Job Targets

jist Works
America's Career Publisher

OVERNIGHT CAREER CHOICE, Second Edition

© 2011 by JIST Publishing and Michael Farr

Published by JIST Works, an imprint of JIST Publishing
7321 Shadeland Station, Suite 200
Indianapolis, Indiana 46256-3923

Phone: 800-648-JIST
E-mail: info@jist.com

Fax: 877-454-7839
Web site: www.jist.com

Visit our Web site at **www.jist.com** for information on JIST, free job search information, tables of contents, sample pages, and ordering information on our many products.

Quantity discounts are available for JIST books. Please call our Sales Department at 800-648-JIST or visit www.jist.com for a free catalog and more information.

Acquisitions Editor: Susan Pines
Development Editor: Stephanie Koutek
Layout: Toi Davis
Cover Designer: Alan Evans
Proofreaders: Paula Lowell, Jeanne Clark
Indexer: Kelly D. Henthorne

Printed in the United States of America

15 14 13 12 11 10   9 8 7 6 5 4 3 2 1

Library of Congress Cataloging-in-Publication data is on file with the Library of Congress.

ISBN 978-1-59357-810-7

Choose Your Ideal Career Tonight

This small book is designed to quickly make a big difference in your career and your life by helping you discover your career focus.

Many people spend months or years unhappy in their careers. Some move from job to job, always searching for more-fulfilling or better-paying work. Others say they "fell into" a career without asking if it suited them. Still others follow in the footsteps of a parent, take any available job, or pursue a hot new field. These paths work out for some people, of course. But many others never discover their true career interests and are dissatisfied with work.

According to research, most people can expect three to five career changes during their working years and ten or more job changes. In addition, only half of all workers are happy with their jobs. These indicators show a clear need for more careful career planning both now and throughout our working lives.

Fortunately, through a proven process and some current facts on jobs, this book helps you pinpoint your ideal career without wasting time and energy. Is it that easy and quick to find your career fit? The answer is "Yes!" This book shows you how. Start with the introduction for guidance in getting the most from this book in a short time.

Contents

A Brief Introduction to Using This Book 1

Follow a Proven Process for Making a Good Career Choice 1

You Don't Have to Read All Night 1

Chapter 1: Quick But Important Points About Career Choice 5

Defining Your "Ideal" Job Is Tricky 5

Clarifying What You Want to Do Involves More Than
Choosing a Job Title 6

Most People Want More Than Money from Work 7

The Nine Most Important Components of an Ideal Job 10

The Role of Education and Training in Career Choice 11

Career Management Is a Lifelong Process 14

Incorporate Life Planning into Your Career Choice 15

Key Points: Chapter 1 16

Chapter 2: What Are You Good At? 17

Learn the Three Types of Skills 17

Identify Your Skills 18

Translate Your Knowledge of Your Skills to Your
Career Choice 41

Key Points: Chapter 2 41

Chapter 3: What Interests You? 43

Review 16 Career Interest Areas 43

Look Closely at Career Clues for Your Top Interest Areas 50

Key Points: Chapter 3 53

Chapter 4: What Motivates and Is Important to You? ...55

Learn What You Value Most in a Career 55

Rank Your Most Important Values 58

Key Points: Chapter 4 59

Chapter 5: Other Key Considerations When Defining Your Ideal Job 61

How Much Money Do You Want to Make—Or Are You Willing to Accept? 61

How Much Responsibility Are You Willing to Accept? 63

Where Do You Want Your Ideal Job to Be Located—In What City or Region? 64

What Special Knowledge or Interests Would You Like to Use or Pursue? 65

What Sort of Work Environment Do You Prefer? 66

What Types of People Do You Prefer to Work With? 68

You Have Defined Nine Ideal Career Characteristics 69

Key Points: Chapter 5 69

Chapter 6: Finally! Identify Specific Job Titles 71

Why Accurate Information About Specific Jobs Is Important 71

How the Job Descriptions Are Organized 72

Review Job Titles 73

Don't Overlook the End of This Chapter 73

Go Back and Review the Job Descriptions 125

More About the Data in the Job Descriptions 126

What's Next? 128

Key Points: Chapter 6 129

Chapter 7: Identify Industries That Interest You 131

Some Background on Industry Growth 132

Service-Providing Industries Have Accounted for Virtually All Growth 135

Skills Required in Major Industries 136

Review 43 Major Industries 143

Learn More About Targeted Industries 146

Key Points: Chapter 7 148

Chapter 8: Overnight Career Choice Matrix and Action Plan 149

Summarize the Characteristics of Your Ideal Career 150

Put Your Ideal Career Characteristics into Graphic Form with the Career Wheel 152

Brainstorm Combinations with the Overnight Career Choice Matrix 153

Your Ideal Job Definition 156

Your Overnight Career Choice Action Plan.......................... 157

Key Points: Chapter 8... 160

Chapter 9: Write Your Job Objective 161

Avoid a Self-Centered, "Gimme" Approach........................... 161

Sample Job Objectives 161

Five Tips for Writing a Good Job Objective........................... 162

Construct Your Job Objective.. 164

Finalize Your Job Objective 166

A Few Final Comments 166

Key Points: Chapter 9... 167

Appendix A: Job Exploration Worksheet......................169

Appendix B: Sources of More Career Information 173

Major Sources of Job Descriptions and Related Information 174

Other Helpful Career and Education Books........................... 175

Other Research Options 176

Index 177

A Brief Introduction to Using This Book

If you are going to work, you might as well do something you enjoy, are good at, and want to do. Yet many people struggle with finding their career focus.

Are you ready for a career change or maybe your first career? Perhaps you can't seem to find the right job, have lost your job, or want more meaningful work. You could, through trial and error, learn which career suits you best. You could read longer books on the topic. You could take a career interest inventory or other test to narrow your options. Although these efforts may be helpful, they take time, money, and energy. None is guaranteed to give you the insight you need to make a good career choice. Career choice is a complex decision, as Chapter 1 explains.

Follow a Proven Process for Making a Good Career Choice

Fortunately, a proven process for discovering your ideal career exists. This book, in a short period of time, takes you through the key steps in this process. When you finish this book, you will have spent more time planning your career than most people do in a lifetime.

So you deserve applause for picking up this book and for deciding to learn more about your career options. The time you spend is very likely to pay off in career success and satisfaction for years to come.

You Don't Have to Read All Night

You can get through this book by working through it today, sleeping on what you learn, and finishing up tomorrow. (You don't need to stay up all night unless you want to!) Just follow this roadmap to get the most from this book:

1. **Read the table of contents.** It introduces you to the content of the book and its chapters.

2. **Learn the most important points about career choice by skimming Chapter 1.** Read the opening paragraphs and the sections that sound most interesting to you in Chapter 1. Pay special attention to the section called "The Nine Most Important Components of an Ideal Job." You can read the entire chapter in detail later if you want.

3. **Gain insight into your key skills by completing the checklists and worksheets in Chapter 2.** This chapter may take more time to get through than the other chapters will. But the results are worth it because knowing what you are good at is an essential part of choosing a career. Unless you use the skills you enjoy and are good at, it is unlikely you will be fully satisfied in your career.

4. **Discover what interests you most by reviewing the 16 career interest areas described in Chapter 3.** Identify the career clusters that interest you most. This step helps you more clearly identify specific careers to consider in Chapter 6.

5. **Consider your key work values and motivators in Chapter 4.** This short chapter presents a checklist of values that give people the most satisfaction and success. Work values include creativity, stability, independence, good pay, good co-workers, and a sense of accomplishment.

6. **Review six other factors important in your ideal career in Chapter 5.** These factors include preferred earnings, level of responsibility desired, preferred location, special knowledge that you would like to use in your career, desired work environment, and the types of people you would like to work with and for.

7. **Review major job titles and job descriptions for your key career interest areas.** Chapter 6 is lengthy, but you don't need to read it all. Instead, under your top career interest areas (identified in Chapter 3), skim the jobs and check out those that sound most interesting.

8. **Pinpoint the industries that interest you the most in Chapter 7.** The industry you work in is often as important as what job you choose because of pay, stability, your interest in it, and other factors. Use the checklist in this chapter to learn which industries suit you best.

9. **Put your ideal career choice into words in Chapter 8.** Focus on completing the "Overnight Career Choice Matrix" and "Your Ideal Job Definition."

By following the preceding suggestions, you will target the most important questions in career choice, get to know yourself a little better, and clearly define your career focus. Chapter 9 helps you write your job objective when you're ready to begin your job search.

So what are you waiting for? Jump right in and find your career focus!

Chapter 1

Quick But Important Points About Career Choice

People often approach career choice with the assumption that they are looking for a particular job title. This is a sensible approach, and this book helps you pinpoint the job titles that suit you best. But this book also helps you consider other factors, in addition to a job title, to help you define your *ideal* job.

For example, what interests do you have, what industry would you like to work in, with what sorts of people, and in what sort of an organization? The answers to these and other questions can be *very* important to you for many reasons yet often are not given much consideration.

This chapter introduces the nine most important factors to consider in defining your ideal job. It also helps you explore the role that education and training play in your career choice. Chapter 6 helps you research specific job titles that match your current or future needs and wishes.

Defining Your "Ideal" Job Is Tricky

Defining your ideal job is tricky business. You might start by trying to identify a job title that suits you—for example, salesworker, computer technician, chef, or teacher. But consider that the U.S. Department of Labor has formal written descriptions for *hundreds* of job titles. This is far too many jobs for anyone to know well enough to evaluate. Add to that the many substantial differences among employers and work environments and the choices quickly become overwhelming. You might be delighted to work in one place and miserable working in another, yet both jobs could have the same job title and look much the same on paper.

Your ideal job is more complex and specific to you and your needs than any one job title.

Clarifying What You Want to Do Involves More Than Choosing a Job Title

Most people don't take the time to clarify what they have to offer or what they want to do. They focus their career planning on a job title similar to one they had in the past or that is related to their education or training. Rather than analyze what they really want to do, they pursue what they believe they are qualified for. All too often, people choose a job title and then put it on their resume or job applications as their job objective.

While your ideal job and your job *objective* are not exactly the same thing, let's consider job objectives, because most people are familiar with them. In addition, a well-done job objective contains many elements that are similar to an ideal career definition.

Here is an example of a nicely written job objective from someone's resume: "A position requiring skills in organizing, communicating, and dealing with people. Prefer a small- to mid-size organization engaged in creative activities. Background in office management. Skilled in word processing, spreadsheets, Internet research, and other computer operations."

> **Note:** *A job objective focuses on what you can do for the employer. Your ideal career definition covers similar points but includes the things that you want, such as good pay, a short commute, and friendly co-workers. Chapter 9 covers job objectives in detail.*

Although it doesn't mention a job title, this is just the sort of thing that a person who has worked as an administrative assistant or other office position might write on a resume. It mentions skills and preferences without limiting job choices.

This sample job objective would allow this person to be considered for a wide variety of jobs and not be limited to a specific job called administrative assistant. Other jobs this person might do include the following:

- Office manager
- Sales associate
- Customer service representative
- Receptionist

- Researcher

- Human resources assistant

- Web site coordinator

Do you see how your options expand when you consider not just a job title, but also the type of work, employer, and work environment you prefer? So don't limit yourself by choosing just a job title and setting that as your goal—either in your head or on your resume. Instead, be clear about what you want and have to offer and seek an employer who will allow you to do a job that fits those interests and skills.

> **Tip:** *A good career choice involves more than deciding on a job title. For example, if you have training in accounting but have great interest in fashion design, can you think of a career that might combine these two things? Or what if you are a computer repair technician but also enjoy selling? You can combine these things—and other factors important to you—in a job.*

Most People Want More Than Money from Work

For most of human history, a high percentage of people were not happy in their jobs. Most of them were stuck in the same work roles as their parents, with few opportunities for change. Nowadays, we have more opportunities, but many people are still unhappy with their jobs. According to a recent survey by the Conference Board, a New York–based business research group, more than half of workers feel this way.

But perhaps some of today's dissatisfaction is explained by raised expectations. That is, many people now look for both meaning and enjoyment from the way they earn their livings. They want more than simply earning a paycheck.

If you're like many people, the type of work you do and the people you work with are more important to your job satisfaction than pay. In addition, you are more likely to enjoy, stay in, and be successful at a career that suits your interests and skills. For these reasons, you would be wise to spend some time considering what you want out of your work.

Money Is Important, But Other Things Are More Important

A study by the Gallup Poll indicated that 78 percent of those surveyed rated "interesting work" as very important for job satisfaction. Only one measure, "good health insurance and other benefits," was rated higher. While many people value making good money (particularly those who don't make enough to live reasonably well), only 56 percent rated "high income" as being very important to them. It's not that money isn't important. It's just that most working people value other things, too. The table that follows shows other things that were rated higher than money.

What Makes People Satisfied with Their Jobs

Factor	Percentage of People Rating as Important
Good health insurance and other benefits	80
Interesting work	78
Job security	78
Opportunity to learn new skills	68
Having a week or more of vacation	66
Being able to work independently	64
Recognition from co-workers	62
Regular hours, no weekends or nights	58
Being able to help others	58
Limiting job stress	58
High income	56

The next table shows the results of another survey, this one by Louis Harris and Associates, asking people to rate those things they considered to be very important in their work. Again, money comes up as important, but not as important as some other things.

What People Say Is Very Important in Their Work

Factor	Percentage of People Rating as Important
A challenging job	82
Good benefits	80
Good pay	74
Free exchange of information	74
Chance to make significant contributions	74
The right to privacy	62

The final table presents the results of a survey taken by Research & Forecasts. It asked people to rate various work factors and select their two most important choices. The percentages indicate those who selected each item among their highest two work-related values. It makes sense that those with lower levels of education rate money as most important, because they are likely to earn less than those with more education. But more than 50 percent of those with a high school diploma or less education picked other things as more important than pay alone.

Work Values Differ by Level of Education

Factor	Percentage selecting factor among two most important		
	High School Graduate or Less	Some College	College Graduate
Pay	46	42	29
Amount of independence	31	35	40
Pleasant working conditions	30	23	17
Liking the people at work	29	24	19
Gratifying work	25	32	43
Contribution to the public good	11	14	23
Important career step	10	15	19

The Nine Most Important Components of an Ideal Job

Many experts have given a lot of thought to the factors you should consider when selecting a job. A large body of research provides predictors for career satisfaction and success, with great differences in opinion on what approach is most valid or which factors are most important in a career choice.

Following are nine factors that play key roles in defining your ideal job. These factors are based on research by vocational psychologists who have identified the most important things to consider in defining your ideal career.

> **Tip:** *Most people don't think about the following factors in an organized way. Yet these very things help you find your true career focus and make a huge difference in your long-term career satisfaction and success.*

Nine Key Factors to Consider in Planning Your Career

1. Skills and abilities
2. Interests
3. Personal values
4. Preferred earnings
5. Level of responsibility
6. Location
7. Special knowledge
8. Work environment
9. Types of people you like to work with and for

You may have noticed that what is *not* included in the list is a job title. That can come later, after the other factors are clearly defined.

The chapters that follow help you pinpoint the characteristics of your ideal job by exploring what you really want in terms of your interests, values, skills, and other preferences. In addition, brief descriptions of 288 jobs and job-growth facts about 43 industries help you further explore possible career options.

The Role of Education and Training in Career Choice

Too many people think that after they finish their formal education, they are set for life. Not so. No matter how much education or training you have, you may need more to change, advance, and succeed in your career. Even if you stay in your current field and just fine-tune your career focus, you most likely will need training to keep up with changes in technology, increase your productivity, upgrade your skills, and get promoted.

Don't let the need for more education hold you back from your ideal job. You may not need to complete a traditional college degree program. Many other education and training options are available today, including short-term certificate programs, online learning, night school, internships, learning through volunteer work, and accelerated programs. You can be on your way to a new career sooner than you may think.

Education and Earnings Are Closely Related

Although earnings are not the most important thing to most workers, your salary affects your life. If you want a higher salary, you'll need higher-level skills and more training and education.

Most people understand that level of education is related to earnings, but many don't realize how substantial the differences are. Following are the earnings by level of education as released by the U.S. Department of Labor. For each level, you can see the dollar and percent premium of pay over those who dropped out of high school.

Annual 2009 Earnings for Full-Time Workers Ages 25 and Older, by Educational Attainment			
Education Level	Earnings Per Year	Earnings Premium Over High School Dropouts	Percentage of Earnings Over High School Dropouts
Some high school, no diploma	$23,600	—	—
High school diploma/GED	$32,600	$9,000	38
Some college, no degree	$36,300	$12,700	54

(continued)

(continued)

Education Level	Earnings Per Year	Earnings Premium Over High School Dropouts	Percentage of Earnings Over High School Dropouts
Associate degree	$39,600	$16,000	68
Bachelor's degree	$53,300	$29,700	126
Master's degree	$65,400	$41,800	177
Doctorate	$79,700	$56,100	238
Professional degree	$79,500	$55,900	237

When you look at the numbers, it's clear that additional education pays off at all levels. The average high school graduate earns $9,000 more (or 38 percent more) than the average high school dropout. A four-year college graduate earns $20,700 more than a high school graduate. This means that, over a decade, a college graduate will earn about $207,000 more than someone with a high school diploma. That is enough to make a big difference in lifestyle and more than enough to pay off any cost of the education itself. Over a 40-year work life, the difference in earnings is staggering. The average college graduate will earn well over a million dollars more than a high school graduate after inflation is considered.

> **Note:** *Average earnings can be misleading because many workers earn much more or much less than the average. Also, some high school dropouts earn much more than the average for college graduates.*

Education and Job Security Are Also Closely Related

You say you want more from your job than just a paycheck? No matter what satisfactions you expect to get from your job, you won't get them unless you *have* a job. That's why you should consider the close relationship between education and job security.

It turns out that a higher level of education also tends to result in a lower level of unemployment. Here are the 2009 unemployment rates by level of education as released by the U.S. Department of Labor. For each level, you can see the percent difference over those who dropped out of high school.

Unemployment Rate in 2009 for Full-Time Workers Ages 25 and Older, by Educational Attainment		
Education Level	Unemployment Rate	Percentage of Employment Premium Over High School Dropouts
Some high school, no diploma	14.6	—
High school diploma/GED	9.7	4.9
Some college, no degree	8.6	6.0
Associate degree	6.8	7.8
Bachelor's degree	5.2	9.4
Master's degree	3.9	10.7
Doctorate	2.5	12.1
Professional degree	2.3	12.3

You'll find similar results if you look at the percentages of workers who are working part time but want to work full time. Workers with more education are less likely to be in that unhappy position.

More Education Does Not Guarantee Success

Less unemployment at higher pay—sounds like a good deal, doesn't it? Nevertheless, success is not guaranteed.

Many college graduates are not unemployed but are *underemployed,* which means they are holding a job that doesn't require their college degree. Some of those counted as underemployed chose to be so while they attended graduate school or spent their time in other ways, but many were unable to find better jobs due to competition or other factors.

So a college degree does not guarantee success in the job market. About one in five new grads initially has to accept a job that is not typically held by grads. Eventually, more than 90 percent of new graduates find jobs typically held by college graduates.

Trade and Technical Training Are Alternatives to a Four-Year College Degree

Although more education clearly pays off in the job market, you should note that college is not the only route to higher earnings. Many trade, technical, sales, and other fields offer similar opportunities to those without a college degree. A well-trained plumber, auto mechanic, chef, computer repair technician, police officer, tool and die maker, or medical technologist can do quite well in our economy.

> **Tip:** *While having a college degree is clearly a good thing, jobs requiring a two-year associate degree are growing the fastest of all, and many of these jobs are in high-wage health-care and technical areas.*

These and many other occupations require one to four years of specialized training, and many apprenticeship programs provide on-the-job training while paying you wages. Outstanding people in sales, small business, management, self-employment, and other activities can still do quite well without a college degree, although more education is often required to compete for the better positions.

Career Management Is a Lifelong Process

No matter how thoughtfully you choose your career goal now, your career will most likely change over the course of your life. Some experts estimate that the average person will change careers three to five times and change jobs ten or more times during their working years.

That is a lot of change, which makes it important for you to know what you are particularly good at doing and develop those skills throughout your life. As your interests change or new job opportunities arise, you may choose to develop new skills or emphasize existing ones in new and creative ways.

Career Change Versus Job Change

A career change is a change in the type of work you do. A job change involves moving from one employer to another—and doing a similar job for both—but a career change is a more substantial change.

If you waited on tables in a restaurant when going to school, and then got a job as a medical technician when you graduated, that would be a change in career (as well as a change in employer, of course). Another example of a career change is when a teacher leaves the educational system and becomes a real estate agent.

This ongoing activity is called *career management*. If you were a business manager, you would have a business plan worked out when you started your business, but you would never stop making decisions and changes to your plans to keep the business running profitably. In the same way, you will never be finished making decisions and plans about your career. As you learn and experience more, and as new opportunities arise, you will probably revise your career plans, moving from one job or one career to another. This book helps you develop the skills to make the best career management choices throughout your life.

Incorporate Life Planning into Your Career Choice

Your current priority may be to find a new or better career. That is a worthy objective. Before you begin the search for your ideal career, however, define clearly what you want and need from a job. Be certain to consider how that job might help you get where you want to go with your life.

Look for Some Meaning in Your Work

Good career management is extremely important, but it should be done in the context of what you want to do with your life. How can you, for example, incorporate elements of pleasure and learning into your next job?

Earning a living can be a difficult task. People sometimes hold jobs that they do not enjoy just to "get by." But consider that having fun, having meaningful relationships, helping other people, and finding satisfaction and meaning from what we do with our lives is what life is all about. So look for joy in your life and your job and for some meaning in your life's work.

This chapter has outlined a few points that help you discover your ideal job. There is a lot to think about, and it may seem a bit overwhelming to make a decision to go in one career direction over another. But the stakes are very high for you, both in money and in personal satisfaction.

Key Points: Chapter 1

- Defining your ideal career involves more than just choosing a job title.

- You are more likely to enjoy, stay in, and be successful at a career that suits your interests and skills.

- Nine factors are important when defining your ideal job: skills and abilities, interests, personal values, preferred earnings, level of responsibility, location, special knowledge, work environment, and types of people you like to work with and for.

- Education and training usually play an important role in future earnings and job security.

- Career management is a lifelong process, and your career choice may change several times as you or your opportunities do.

Chapter 2

What Are You Good At?

The first key factor or step in defining your ideal career is knowing your best skills and abilities. This chapter helps you identify the skills you have and begin to develop a "skills language" that is tremendously important for your career choice, your job search, and—more importantly—your life.

Knowing what you are good at is an essential part of choosing a career. Unless you use the skills that you enjoy using and are good at, it is unlikely that you will be fully satisfied in your job.

Most people are not good at recognizing and listing the skills they have, and very few people can quickly itemize the specific skills that are needed for success in the job they want.

Lack of understanding about skills not only leads to job dissatisfaction; it also may prevent you from getting hired. You need to be able to explain to employers why you have the skills required for the job. But according to one survey of employers, more than 90 percent of the people they interview cannot adequately do this. The job applicants may have the necessary skills, but they can't communicate that fact.

Learn the Three Types of Skills

Many people don't realize that everyone has hundreds of skills, not just a few.

Simple skills such as closing your fingers to grip a pen are building blocks for more complex skills, such as writing a sentence, and even more complex skills, such as writing a book.

Among your hundreds of skills, some will be more important to an employer than others. Some will be far more important to *you* in deciding what sort of job you want. To simplify the task of skill identification, it's useful to think of skills in three major categories: adaptive skills, transferable skills, and job-related skills.

Adaptive Skills/Personality Traits

You probably take for granted the many skills you use every day to survive and function. These skills can be called adaptive skills because they allow you to adapt or adjust to a variety of situations. Such skills, which are highly valued by employers, include getting to work on time, honesty, enthusiasm, and getting along with others. In young people, they're sometimes called *workplace readiness* skills because they're so important that youngsters aren't ready to be workers until they've mastered these skills. Who would hire someone who can't show up on time?

Transferable Skills

Transferable skills are general skills that can be useful in a variety of jobs. They can be transferred from one job—or even one career—to another. For example, writing clearly, speaking clearly, doing simple arithmetic, and being able to organize and prioritize tasks would be desirable skills in many jobs.

Job-Related Skills

These are the skills people typically think of first when asked, "Do you have any skills?" They are related to a particular job or type of job. An auto mechanic, for example, needs to know how to tune engines and repair brakes. Other jobs also have job-specific skills required for that job in addition to the adaptive and transferable skills needed to succeed in almost any job.

> **Note:** *This system of dividing skills into three categories is not perfect. Some things, such as being trustworthy, dependable, and well-organized, are really not skills as much as they are personality traits that can be acquired. There is also some overlap between the three skills categories. For example, a skill such as being organized might be considered either adaptive or transferable.*

Identify Your Skills

Because being aware of your skills is so important, this chapter includes a series of checklists and other activities to help you identify your key skills. Recognizing these skills is important so that you will select jobs that you will do well in. Developing a skills language can also be very helpful to you when you write resumes and conduct a job search. To begin, answer the question in the box on the next page.

WHAT MAKES ME A GOOD WORKER?

On the following lines, list three things about yourself that you think make you a good worker. Take your time. Think about what an employer might like about you or the way you work.

1. _____

2. _____

3. _____

The skills you just wrote down may be among the most important things to consider in your career choice. They may also be among the most important things that employers will want to know about you.

Most (but not all) people write adaptive skills when asked this question. Next, let's get a more complete understanding of which adaptive skills you're good at.

Identify Your Adaptive Skills and Personality Traits

Following is a list of adaptive skills that tend to be important in defining a person's ideal career as well as being important to employers. The ones listed as "The Minimum" are those that most employers consider essential for job survival, and many will not hire someone who has problems in these areas.

Look over the list and put a check mark next to each adaptive skill that you possess. Put a second check mark next to those skills that are particularly important for you to use or include in your next job.

ADAPTIVE SKILLS CHECKLIST

The Minimum

___Have good attendance   ___Meet deadlines

___Am honest   ___Get along with supervisor

___Arrive on time   ___Get along with co-workers

___Follow instructions   ___Am hardworking, productive

(continued)

(continued)

Other Adaptive Skills

___Able to coordinate	___Intuitive	___Solve problems
___Results-oriented	___Decisive	___Team player
___Mentor others	___Work well with diversity	___Multitask
___Friendly	___Discreet	___Patient
___Ambitious	___Learn quickly	___Spontaneous
___Good-natured	___Eager	___Persistent
___Assertive	___Loyal	___Steady
___Helpful	___Efficient	___Physically strong
___Capable	___Mature	___Tactful
___Humble	___Energetic	___Practical
___Cheerful	___Methodical	___Take pride in work
___Imaginative	___Enthusiastic	___Competent
___Modest	___Reliable	___Independent
___Expressive	___Tenacious	___Well organized
___Motivated	___Resourceful	___Industrious
___Flexible	___Thrifty	___Natural
___Responsible	___Conscientious	___Formal
___Trustworthy	___Informal	___Open-minded
___Self-confident	___Creative	___Optimistic
___Versatile	___Intelligent	___Sincere
___Sense of humor	___Dependable	___Original

Other Adaptive Skills You Have

Add any adaptive skills that were not listed but that you think are important on the job:

_____

_____

_____

_____

_____

_____

Your Top Adaptive Skills

Carefully review the checklist you just completed and select the three adaptive skills that you most want to use in your next job. These three skills are *extremely* important to include in your ideal career choice, on your resume, and in job interviews.

1. _____

2. _____

3. _____

Identify Your Transferable Skills

The checklist that follows features transferable skills—that is, skills needed for success on a wide variety of jobs.

The skills listed as "Key Transferable Skills" are the most important ones. They often are required in jobs with more responsibility and higher pay, so you should emphasize these skills if you have them.

The remaining transferable skills are grouped into categories that may be helpful to you. Go ahead and check each skill you are strong in, and then double-check the skills you want to use in your next job. When you are finished, you should have checked 10 to 20 skills at least once.

TRANSFERABLE SKILLS CHECKLIST

Key Transferable Skills

___Meet deadlines

___Plan

___Speak in public

___Control budgets

___Meet the public

___Negotiate

___Instruct others

___Organize or manage projects

___Solve problems

___Manage money or budgets

___Manage people

___Supervise others

___Increase sales or efficiency

___Accept responsibility

___Write

___Use computers or other technology

Dealing with Data

___Analyze data or facts

___Investigate

___Audit records

___Keep financial records

___Budget

___Locate answers or information

___Calculate, compute

___Manage money

___Classify data

___Negotiate

___Compare, inspect, or record facts

___Count, observe, compile

___Research

___Pay attention to detail

___Use technology to analyze data

___Evaluate

___Take inventory

___Synthesize

Working with People

___Administer

___Be patient

___Care for others

___Be pleasant

___Counsel people

___Be sensitive

___Be diplomatic

___Supervise

___Help others

___Persuade   ___Demonstrate   ___Be tactful

___Confront others   ___Be sociable   ___Have insight

___Teach   ___Be tough   ___Understand

___Interview others   ___Listen   ___Be outgoing

___Be tolerant   ___Trust   ___Be kind

___Negotiate

Using Words, Ideas

___Be articulate   ___Correspond with others

___Edit   ___Invent

___Speak in public   ___Communicate verbally

___Remember information   ___Create new ideas

___Write clearly   ___Think logically

___Research   ___Be ingenious

Leadership

___Arrange social functions   ___Direct others

___Motivate people   ___Exercise self-control

___Be competitive   ___Explain things to others

___Negotiate agreements   ___Motivate yourself

___Make decisions   ___Get results

___Plan   ___Solve problems

___Delegate   ___Mediate problems

___Run meetings   ___Take risks

Creative, Artistic

___Be artistic   ___Perform, act

___Appreciate music   ___Draw

___Present artistic ideas   ___Play instruments

(continued)

(continued)

___Express yourself   ___Dance

___Design

Other Transferable Skills

___Drive or operate vehicles   ___Assemble or make things

___Build, observe, inspect things   ___Construct or repair buildings

Other Transferable Skills You Have

Add any transferable skills that were not listed but that you think are important:

_____

_____

_____

_____

_____

Your Top Transferable Skills

Select the five top transferable skills you have that you want to use in your next job and list them here:

1. _____

2. _____

3. _____

4. _____

5. _____

The Skills Employers Want

As an indication of the importance of adaptive and transferable skills, consider the results of a survey of employers. The study, called "Workplace Basics—The Skills Employers Want," was conducted jointly by the U.S. Department of Labor and the American Association of Counseling and Development.

It turns out that most of the skills they want are either adaptive or transferable skills. Of course, specific job-related skills remain important, but basic skills form an essential foundation for success on the job. Here are the top skills employers identified:

1. Learning to learn
2. Basic academic skills in reading, writing, and computation
3. Good communication skills, including listening and speaking
4. Creative thinking and problem solving
5. Self-esteem, motivation, and goal setting
6. Personal and career development skills
7. Interpersonal/negotiation skills and teamwork
8. Organizational effectiveness and leadership

What is most interesting is that most of these skills are not formally taught in school. Of course, job-specific skills are also important (an accountant will still need to know accounting), but the adaptive and transferable skills are the ones that allow you to succeed in any job.

Again, this study shows the importance of being aware of your skills and using them well in career planning. If you have any weaknesses in one or more of the skills that were listed, consider how you can improve them. And let your *awareness* of any weakness be a strength. For example, if you don't have a specific skill that's required for a job, let the employer know that you don't but add that you are eager to learn and you are a quick study. This comment shows the employer that you are not afraid of learning new skills and that you are confident in your abilities. Furthermore, if you are already strong in one or more of the top skills employers want, look for opportunities to develop and use them in your work.

Identify Your Job-Related Skills

Many jobs require skills that are specific to that occupation. Airline pilots obviously need to know how to fly an airplane; good adaptive and transferable skills are not enough to be considered for that job.

People gain job-related skills in various ways, including education, training, work, hobbies, and other life experiences. In the worksheets that follow, you'll take stock of your skills and accomplishments. Pay special attention to those experiences that you really enjoyed. These experiences often demonstrate skills that you should try to use in your career choice.

When possible, quantify your activities or results with numbers to prove your accomplishments. Employers relate more easily to percentages, numbers, and ratios than to quality terms such as more, many, greater, less, fewer, and so on. For example, saying "presented to groups as large as 200 people" has more impact than "did many presentations."

EDUCATION AND TRAINING WORKSHEET

We spend many years in school and learn more lessons there than you might at first realize. For example, in our early years of schooling we acquire basic skills that are important in most jobs: getting along with others, reading instructions, and accepting supervision. Later on, courses become more specialized and relevant to potential careers.

This worksheet helps you review your education and training experiences, even those that may have occurred years ago. Some courses may seem more important to certain careers than others. But keep in mind that even the courses that don't seem to support a particular career choice can be an important source of skills.

Elementary School Experiences

While few employers will ask you about these years, jot down any highlights of things you felt particularly good about; doing so may help you identify important interests and directions to consider for the future. For example, note the following:

Subjects that you did well in or that might relate to your ideal career:

_____

_____

Extracurricular activities/hobbies/leisure activities:

_____

_____

Accomplishments/things you did well (in or out of school):

_____

_____

High School Experiences

These experiences will be more important for a recent graduate and less so for those with college, work, or other life experiences. But, whatever your situation, what you did during these years can give you important clues to use in your career choice.

Name of school(s)/years attended:

_____

Subjects you did well in or might relate to your ideal career:

_____

_____

_____

Extracurricular activities/hobbies/leisure activities:

_____

_____

_____

Accomplishments/things you did well (in or out of school):

_____

_____

_____

_____

_____

_____

Postsecondary Training or College Experiences

If you graduated from a two- or four-year college, took college classes, or attended other formal training or education programs after high school, what you learned and did during this time will be important for your career choice and of interest to employers. Emphasize here those things that you think directly support your ability to do a job.

(continued)

(continued)

Name of school(s)/years attended:

_____

_____

Major:

_____

Courses related to a job:

_____

_____

_____

_____

Extracurricular activities/hobbies/leisure activities:

_____

_____

_____

_____

Accomplishments/things you did well (in or out of school):

_____

_____

_____

_____

_____

Specific things you learned or can do that may relate to your career choice:

_____

_____

_____

_____

Additional Training and Education

There are many formal and informal ways to learn, and some of the most important things are often learned outside of the classroom. Use this worksheet to list any additional training or education that might relate to your career choice. Include military training, on-the-job training, workshops, or any other formal or informal training you have had. You can also include any substantial learning you obtained through a hobby, family activities, online research, or similar informal source.

Names of courses or programs/dates taken/any certificates or credentials earned:

_____

_____

_____

_____

_____

_____

Specific things you learned or can do that relate to the job you want:

_____

_____

_____

_____

_____

_____

THE JOB AND VOLUNTEER HISTORY WORKSHEET

Use this worksheet to list each major job you have held and the information related to each. Begin with your most recent job, followed by previous ones.

Include military experience and unpaid volunteer work here. Both are work and are particularly important if you do not have much paid civilian work experience. Create additional sheets to cover all of your significant jobs or unpaid experiences as needed. If you have been promoted, consider handling the new position as a separate job from the original position.

Whenever possible, provide numbers to support what you did: number of people served over one or more years, number of transactions processed, percent sales increase, total inventory value you were responsible for, payroll of the staff you supervised, total budget you were responsible for, and other specific data.

Job 1

Name of organization: _____

Address: _____

Job title(s): _____

Employed from _____ to_____

Computer, software, or other machinery or equipment you used:

_____

_____

_____

Data, information, or reports you created or used:

_____

_____

_____

People-oriented duties or responsibilities to co-workers, customers, others:

_____

_____

_____

_____

_____

Services you provided or products you produced:

_____

_____

_____

_____

_____

Reasons for promotions or salary increases, if any:

_____

_____

_____

_____

_____

Details on anything you did to help the organization, such as increase productivity, improve procedures or processes, simplify or reorganize job duties, decrease costs, increase profits, improve working conditions, reduce turnover, or other improvements. Quantify results when possible—for example, "Increased order processing by 50 percent, with no increase in staff costs."

_____

_____

(continued)

(continued)

Specific things you learned or can do that you would like to include in your ideal job:

_____

_____

_____

_____

_____

What would your supervisor say about you?

_____

_____

_____

_____

_____

Supervisor's name: _____

Phone number: _____ E-mail address:_____

Job 2

Name of organization: _____

Address: _____

Job title(s): _____

Employed from _____ to_____

Computer, software, or other machinery or equipment you used:

_____

_____

_____

© JIST Works

Data, information, or reports you created or used:

_____

_____

_____

People-oriented duties or responsibilities to co-workers, customers, others:

_____

_____

_____

_____

_____

Services you provided or products you produced:

_____

_____

_____

_____

Reasons for promotions or salary increases, if any:

_____

_____

_____

_____

_____

Details on anything you did to help the organization, such as increase productivity, improve procedures or processes, simplify or reorganize job duties, decrease costs, increase profits, improve working conditions, reduce turnover, or other improvements. Quantify results when possible—for example, "Increased order processing by 50 percent, with no increase in staff costs."

(continued)

(continued)

_____

_____

Specific things you learned or can do that you would like to include in your ideal job:

_____

_____

_____

_____

_____

What would your supervisor say about you?

_____

_____

_____

_____

_____

Supervisor's name: _____

Phone number: _____ E-mail address:_____

Job 3

Name of organization:_____

Address:_____

Job title(s): _____

Employed from _____ to_____

Computer, software, or other machinery or equipment you used:

_____

_____

_____

Data, information, or reports you created or used:

_____

_____

_____

People-oriented duties or responsibilities to co-workers, customers, others:

_____

_____

_____

_____

_____

Services you provided or products you produced:

_____

_____

_____

_____

_____

Reasons for promotions or salary increases, if any:

_____

_____

_____

_____

_____

Details on anything you did to help the organization, such as increase productivity, improve procedures or processes, simplify or reorganize job duties, decrease costs, increase profits, improve working conditions, reduce turnover, or other improvements. Quantify results when possible—for example, "Increased order processing by 50 percent, with no increase in staff costs."

(continued)

(continued)

_____

_____

Specific things you learned or can do that you would like to include in your ideal job:

_____

_____

_____

_____

What would your supervisor say about you?

_____

_____

_____

_____

Supervisor's name: _____

Phone number: _____ E-mail address: _____

Job 4

Name of organization: _____

Address: _____

Job title(s): _____

Employed from _____ to _____

Computer, software, or other machinery or equipment you used:

_____

_____

_____

Data, information, or reports you created or used:

_____

_____

_____

People-oriented duties or responsibilities to co-workers, customers, others:

_____

_____

_____

_____

_____

Services you provided or products you produced:

_____

_____

_____

_____

_____

Reasons for promotions or salary increases, if any:

_____

_____

_____

_____

_____

Details on anything you did to help the organization, such as increase productivity, improve procedures or processes, simplify or reorganize job duties, decrease costs, increase profits, improve working conditions, reduce turnover, or other improvements. Quantify results when possible—for example, "Increased order processing by 50 percent, with no increase in staff costs."

(continued)

(continued)

_____

_____

Specific things you learned or can do that you would like to include in your ideal job:

_____

_____

_____

_____

_____

What would your supervisor say about you?

_____

_____

_____

_____

_____

Supervisor's name: _____

Phone number: _____ E-mail address:_____

OTHER LIFE EXPERIENCES WORKSHEET

Many people overlook how informal life experiences can be important sources of learning or accomplishment. This worksheet is here to encourage you to think about any hobbies or interests you have had—family responsibilities, recreational activities, travel, or any other experiences in your life where you feel some sense of accomplishment. Write any experiences that seem particularly meaningful to you and name the key skills you think were involved.

Situation 1

Describe situation and skills used:

_____

_____

_____

_____

_____

Specific things you learned or can do that you would like to be part of your ideal job:

_____

_____

_____

_____

_____

Situation 2

Describe situation and skills used:

_____

_____

_____

_____

_____

(continued)

(continued)

Specific things you learned or can do that you would like to be part of your ideal job:

_____

_____

_____

_____

_____

Situation 3

Describe situation and skills used:

_____

_____

_____

_____

Specific things you learned or can do that you would like to be part of your ideal job:

_____

_____

_____

_____

_____

Your Top Job-Related Skills

Of all the job-related skills you have, list the most important ones that you would like to include in your ideal career:

1. _____

2. _____

3. _____

4. _____

5. _____

Translate Your Knowledge of Your Skills to Your Career Choice

Knowing the skills you like to use can help you make a better decision about your future career. They are important for an employer to know about, but even more important for you to recognize.

Now that you have an awareness of your skill set, that information will become part of your career focus. Later, in Chapter 8, you will complete an "Overnight Career Choice Matrix" where you can list your best skills.

Key Points: Chapter 2

- Knowing what you are good at is an essential part of choosing a career. Unless you use the skills that you enjoy using and are good at, it is unlikely that you will be fully satisfied in your job.

- Adaptive skills, such as having good work habits and working well with others, are important to employers.

- Transferable skills, which include writing, managing people, and analyzing data, are useful in many careers.

- Job-related skills are those skills you have learned through education, training, and experience.

Chapter 3

What Interests You?

The second important step or factor in defining your ideal career is identifying your interests. Researchers in the field of career development have found that

- Your interests are an important source of information to use in exploring career options.

- You are more likely to be interested in things you are good at, you enjoy doing, or that are important to you.

- Your interests can accurately guide you to explore careers that are most likely to meet your needs.

Review 16 Career Interest Areas

Because exploring thousands of jobs is not practical, researchers at the U.S. Department of Education organized all jobs into 16 interest areas, which are explained in the following checklist. The jobs in each interest area share a basic purpose, kind of employer, or educational preparation, which is why people who find one job interesting also are likely to be interested in other jobs in that area. (These 16 interest areas are often referred to as "career clusters.")

You learn more about specific job titles in Chapter 6. For now, identify your top interests in the "Career Interest Areas Checklist" that follows.

CAREER INTEREST AREAS CHECKLIST

Read the definition of each interest area carefully. For each interest area, put a check mark by the option that best describes your interest in the area: "Not Interested," "Somewhat Interested or Not Sure," or "Very Interested."

1. **Agriculture and Natural Resources.** *An interest in working with plants, animals, forests, or mineral resources for agriculture, horticulture, conservation, extraction, and other purposes.* You can satisfy this interest by working in farming, landscaping, forestry, fishing, mining, and related fields. You may like doing physical work outdoors, such as on a farm or ranch, in a forest, or on a drilling rig. If you have scientific curiosity, you could study plants and animals or analyze biological or rock samples in a lab. If you have management ability, you could own, operate, or manage a fish hatchery, a landscaping business, or a greenhouse.

   ___Not Interested   ___Somewhat Interested or Not Sure
   ___Very Interested

2. **Architecture and Construction.** *An interest in designing, assembling, and maintaining components of buildings and other structures.* You may want to be part of the team of architects, drafters, and others who design buildings and render the plans. If construction interests you, you can find fulfillment in the many building projects that are being undertaken at all times. If you like to organize and plan, you can find careers in managing these projects. Or you can play a more direct role in putting up and finishing buildings by doing jobs such as plumbing, carpentry, masonry, painting, or roofing, either as a skilled craftsworker or as a helper. You can prepare the building site by operating heavy equipment or install, maintain, and repair vital building equipment and systems such as electricity and heating.

   ___Not Interested   ___Somewhat Interested or Not Sure
   ___Very Interested

3. **Arts and Communication.** *An interest in creatively expressing feelings or ideas, in communicating news or information, or*

in performing. You can satisfy this interest in creative, verbal, or performing activities. For example, if you enjoy literature, perhaps writing or editing would appeal to you. Journalism and public relations are other fields for people who like to use their writing or speaking skills. Do you prefer to work in the performing arts? If so, you could direct or perform in drama, music, or dance. If you especially enjoy the visual arts, you could create paintings, sculpture, or ceramics or design products or visual displays. A flair for technology might lead you to specialize in photography, broadcast production, or dispatching.

___Not Interested   ___Somewhat Interested or Not Sure
___Very Interested

4. **Business and Administration.** *An interest in making a business organization or function run smoothly.* You can satisfy this interest by working in a position of leadership or by specializing in a function that contributes to the overall effort in a business, nonprofit organization, or government agency. If you especially enjoy working with people, you may find fulfillment from working in human resources. An interest in numbers may lead you to consider accounting, finance, budgeting, billing, or financial record-keeping. A job as an administrative assistant may interest you if you like a variety of work in a busy environment. If you are good with details and word processing, you may enjoy a job as a secretary or data-entry clerk. Or perhaps you would do well as the manager of a business.

___Not Interested   ___Somewhat Interested or Not Sure
___Very Interested

5. **Education and Training.** *An interest in helping people learn.* You can satisfy this interest by teaching students, who may be preschoolers, retirees, or any age in between. You may specialize in a particular academic field or work with learners of a particular age, with a particular interest, or with a particular learning problem. Working in a library or museum may give you an opportunity to expand people's understanding of the world.

___Not Interested   ___Somewhat Interested or Not Sure
___Very Interested

(continued)

(continued)

6. **Finance and Insurance.** *An interest in helping businesses and people be assured of a financially secure future.* You can satisfy this interest by working in a financial or insurance business in a leadership or support role. If you like gathering and analyzing information, you may find fulfillment as an insurance adjuster or financial analyst. Or you may deal with information at the clerical level as a banking or insurance clerk or in person-to-person situations providing customer service. Another way to interact with people is to sell financial or insurance services that will meet their needs.

___Not Interested ___Somewhat Interested or Not Sure ___Very Interested

7. **Government and Public Administration.** *An interest in helping a government agency serve the needs of the public.* You can satisfy this interest by working in a position of leadership or by specializing in a function that contributes to the role of government. You may help protect the public by working as an inspector or examiner to enforce standards. If you enjoy using clerical skills, you may work as a clerk in a law court or government office. Or perhaps you prefer the top-down perspective of a government executive or urban planner.

___Not Interested ___Somewhat Interested or Not Sure ___Very Interested

8. **Health Science.** *An interest in helping people and animals be healthy.* You can satisfy this interest by working in a health-care team as a doctor, therapist, or nurse. You might specialize in one of the many different parts of the body (such as the teeth or eyes) or in one of the many different types of care. Or you may want to be a generalist who deals with the whole patient. If you like technology, you might find satisfaction working with X-rays or new methods of diagnosis. You might work with healthy people, helping them eat right. If you enjoy working with animals, you might care for them and keep them healthy.

___Not Interested ___Somewhat Interested or Not Sure ___Very Interested

9. **Hospitality, Tourism, and Recreation.** *An interest in catering to the personal wishes and needs of others so that they may enjoy a clean environment, good food and drink, comfortable lodging away from home, and recreation.* You can satisfy this interest by providing services for the convenience, care, and pampering of others in hotels, restaurants, airplanes, beauty parlors, and so on. You may wish to use your love of cooking as a chef. If you like working with people, you may wish to provide personal services by being a travel guide, a flight attendant, a concierge, a hairdresser, or a waiter. You may wish to work in cleaning and building services if you like a clean environment. If you enjoy sports or games, you may work for an athletic team or casino.

___Not Interested   ___Somewhat Interested or Not Sure
___Very Interested

10. **Human Service.** *An interest in improving people's social, mental, emotional, or spiritual well-being.* You can satisfy this interest as a counselor, social worker, or religious worker who helps people sort out their complicated lives or solve personal problems. You may work as a caretaker for very young people or the elderly. Or you may interview people to help identify the social services they need.

___Not Interested   ___Somewhat Interested or Not Sure
___Very Interested

11. **Information Technology.** *An interest in designing, developing, managing, and supporting information systems.* You can satisfy this by working with hardware, software, multimedia, or integrated systems. If you like to use your organizational skills, you might work as an administrator of a system or database. Or you can solve complex problems as a software engineer or systems analyst. If you enjoy getting your hands on the hardware, you might find work servicing computers, peripherals, and information-intense machines such as cash registers and ATMs.

___Not Interested   ___Somewhat Interested or Not Sure
___Very Interested

(continued)

(continued)

12. **Law and Public Safety.** *An interest in upholding people's rights or in protecting people and property by using authority, inspecting, or investigating.* You can satisfy this interest by working in law, law enforcement, fire fighting, the military, and related fields. For example, if you enjoy mental challenge and intrigue, you could investigate crimes or fires for a living. If you enjoy working with verbal and research skills, you may want to defend citizens in court or research deeds, wills, and other legal documents. If you want to help people in critical situations, you may want to fight fires, work as a police officer, or become a paramedic. Or, if you want more routine work in public safety, perhaps a job in guarding, patrolling, or inspecting would appeal to you. If you have management ability, you could seek a leadership position in law enforcement and the protective services. Work in the military gives you a chance to use technical and leadership skills while serving your country.

___Not Interested   ___Somewhat Interested or Not Sure
___Very Interested

13. **Manufacturing.** *An interest in processing materials into intermediate or final products or maintaining and repairing products by using machines or hand tools.* You can satisfy this interest by working in one of many industries that mass-produce goods or by working for a utility that distributes electric power or other resources. You may enjoy manual work, using your hands or hand tools in highly skilled jobs such as assembling engines or electronic equipment. If you enjoy making machines run efficiently or fixing them when they break down, you could seek a job installing or repairing such devices as copiers, aircraft engines, cars, or watches. Perhaps you prefer to set up or operate machines that are used to manufacture products made of food, glass, or paper. You may enjoy cutting and grinding metal and plastic parts to desired shapes and measurements. Or you may want to operate equipment in systems that provide water and process wastewater. You may like inspecting, sorting, counting, or weighing products. Another option is to work with your hands and machinery to move boxes and

freight in a warehouse. If leadership appeals to you, you could manage people engaged in production and repair.

___Not Interested   ___Somewhat Interested or Not Sure
___Very Interested

14. **Retail and Wholesale Sales and Service.** *An interest in bringing others to a particular point of view by personal persuasion and by sales and promotional techniques.* You can satisfy this interest in a variety of jobs that involve persuasion and selling. If you like using your knowledge of science, you may enjoy selling pharmaceutical, medical, or electronic products or services. Real estate offers several kinds of sales jobs as well. If you like speaking on the phone, you could work as a telemarketer. Or you may enjoy selling apparel and other merchandise in a retail setting. If you prefer to help people, you may want a job in customer service.

___Not Interested   ___Somewhat Interested or Not Sure
___Very Interested

15. **Scientific Research, Engineering, and Mathematics.** *An interest in discovering, collecting, and analyzing information about the natural world; in applying scientific research findings to problems in medicine, the life sciences, human behavior, and the natural sciences; in imagining and manipulating quantitative data; and in applying technology to manufacturing, transportation, and other economic activities.* You can satisfy this interest by working with the knowledge and processes of the sciences. You may enjoy researching and developing new knowledge in mathematics, or perhaps solving problems in the physical, life, or social sciences would appeal to you. You may want to study engineering and help create new machines, processes, and structures. If you want to work with scientific equipment and procedures, you could seek a job in a research or testing laboratory.

___Not Interested   ___Somewhat Interested or Not Sure
___Very Interested

16. **Transportation, Distribution, and Logistics.** *An interest in operations that move people or materials.* You can satisfy this

(continued)

(continued)

interest by managing a transportation service, by helping vehicles keep on their assigned schedules and routes, or by driving or piloting a vehicle. If you enjoy taking responsibility, perhaps managing a rail line would appeal to you. If you work well with details and can take pressure on the job, you might consider being an air traffic controller. Or would you rather get out on the highway, on the water, or up in the air? If so, then you could drive a truck from state to state, be employed on a ship, or fly a crop duster over a cornfield. If you prefer to stay closer to home, you could drive a delivery van, taxi, or school bus. You can use your physical strength to load freight and arrange it so it gets to its destination in one piece.

___Not Interested   ___Somewhat Interested or Not Sure
___Very Interested

YOUR TOP INTEREST AREAS

Review each interest area from the previous table. Then write the three to five areas that interest you the most. Don't worry for now whether your choices are practical. Just list the interest areas that you would like to know more about, beginning with the area that interests you most.

1. _____

2. _____

3. _____

4. _____

5. _____

Look Closely at Career Clues for Your Top Interest Areas

Knowing your top interest areas gives you some idea of career areas to explore more carefully. The next worksheet helps you consider three important clues related to the career areas that interest you most. These clues are "Education and Training," "Work Experience," and "Leisure Activities."

Your interests or activities in each of these areas can help you focus your career choice.

✏ CAREER CLUES WORKSHEET

Look at the worksheet that follows. Where indicated, write your top interest areas from the "Your Top Interest Areas" box you just completed.

Now look at the next three columns of the worksheet. At the top of each column is one of the career clues. Use the blank space in each column to write notes related to each interest area you selected. Emphasize related activities you enjoyed or are good at. For example, people who select Agriculture and Natural Resources as a top interest area might write, in the "Education and Training Clues" column, that they liked and did well in biology and natural-science classes. In the "Work Experience Clues" column, they might write that they enjoyed a summer job working with horses at a riding stable. In the "Leisure Activities Clues" column, they might write that they like camping and hiking. Here are some ideas to help you decide what to write for each clue:

- **Education and Training.** Do you have education or training related to this interest? Include formal learning and school course names and informal learning such as reading or on-the-job learning.

- **Work Experience.** Do you have work experience related to this interest? List any paid or unpaid work related to the interest. This can include full- and part-time jobs, volunteer work, work you do at home, and working in a family business.

- **Leisure Activities.** Do you have hobbies or leisure activities related to this interest? Anything you do that is not "work" gives you clues to your real interests. For example, think of magazines you read, clubs and organizations you belong to, extracurricular activities, hobbies, and other related leisure activities.

After you finish with your first interest area, do the same thing for the rest of your interest areas in the list. Instructions for filling in the empty circles come later.

Write Your Top Interest Areas Here	CAREER PLANNING CLUES			Score
	For each clue, write in things you enjoy doing or are good at that relate to each interest area.			
	Education and Training Clues	Work Experience Clues	Leisure Activities Clues	
1.	○	○	○	
2.	○	○	○	
3.	○	○	○	
4.	○	○	○	
5.	○	○	○	

Score Each Interest Area

After you have written your notes in each clue box, total your scores for each interest area. Begin with your first interest area. Under the "Education and Training Clues" column, decide which of the following statements best describes the activities you wrote in that clue box:

1. Activities do not strongly support this interest.

2. Activities provide some support for this interest.

3. Activities provide strong support for this interest.

Now notice the small circles in the lower-right corner of each clue box. This is where you should write the number of the statement you selected. Do this for each clue box for your first interest area. Do the same thing for each clue for the other interest areas. When you are done, add up the numbers you wrote in the three circles for each interest area and put that total in the "Score" column on the right.

What Your Scores Mean

Higher scores usually mean that you have spent more time on or are very interested in that interest area. You may have taken more related classes, spent more leisure time in related activities, or have more directly related work experience. Interest areas with your highest scores are the ones you should consider more closely. They are likely to offer careers that interest you most.

At this point, you have identified groups of careers that interest you most and have eliminated others that are not of interest. Chapter 6 helps you more clearly identify specific jobs within these interest areas to consider now or in the future.

Key Points: Chapter 3

- You are more likely to be interested in things that you are good at, that you enjoy doing, or that are important to you.

- The system of 16 career interest areas, developed by the U.S. Department of Education, helps people explore career and learning options based on interests.

- Your education and training, past work experience, and leisure activities provide important clues to your top career interest areas.

Chapter 4

What Motivates and Is Important to You?

The third important consideration or step in your career choice is your personal values. What are your values? Some people work to help others, and others clean up our environment, build things, make machines work, gain power or prestige, care for animals or plants, or do something else they consider worthwhile. Think about why you might say, at the end of a workday, "That was a good day at work."

Remember the surveys in Chapter 1 that showed that most people want more than money from work? The checklist that follows helps you identify the values to include in your ideal career for the most satisfaction and success.

> **Tip:** *All work is worthwhile if done well. The issue here is just what sorts of things motivate you and are important to you.*

Learn What You Value Most in a Career

This section presents 33 values that many people find important in their jobs.

✎ Work Values Checklist
Read each value and think about how important it is to you. Put a check mark in the column to the right of each value that best indicates how important that value is to include in your career.

(continued)

(continued)

Value	Not Important	Important	Very Important
1. **Help society:** Contribute to the betterment of the world I live in.			
2. **Help others:** Help others directly, either individually or in small groups.			
3. **Public contact:** Have lots of daily contact with people.			
4. **Teamwork/work with others:** Have close working relationships with a group; work as a team toward common goals.			
5. **Competition:** Compete against a goal or other people where there are clear outcomes.			
6. **Have a pleasant work environment:** Be in a work environment I enjoy.			
7. **Be busy:** Have work that keeps me fully occupied and not bored.			
8. **Power and authority:** Have control over other people's work activities; be a manager or supervisor.			
9. **Influence people:** Be in a position to change other people's attitudes and opinions.			
10. **Work alone:** Do things by myself without much contact with or supervision by others.			
11. **Knowledge:** Seek knowledge, truth, and understanding.			
12. **Status:** Be looked up to by others at work and in the community or be recognized as a member of an organization whose work or status is important to me.			
13. **Artistic creativity:** Do creative work in writing, theater, art, design, or any other area.			
14. **General creativity:** Create new ideas, programs, or anything else that is new and different.			
15. **Change and variety:** Have job duties that often change or are done in different settings.			

Value	Not Important	Important	Very Important
16. **Free time:** Have work that allows me to have enough time for family, leisure, and other activities.			
17. **Quality:** Do work that allows me to meet high standards of excellence.			
18. **Stability:** Have job duties that are predictable and not likely to change over a long period of time.			
19. **Security:** Be fairly sure of keeping my job and not having to worry much about losing it.			
20. **Sense of accomplishment:** Have work that allows me to feel I am accomplishing something worthwhile or important.			
21. **Excitement:** Do work that is often exciting.			
22. **Adventure:** Do work that allows me to experience new things and take some risks.			
23. **Good co-workers:** Have a job where I like my co-workers and supervisor.			
24. **Earnings:** Be paid well compared to other workers.			
25. **Advancement:** Have work that allows me to get training, experience, and opportunities to advance in pay and level of responsibility.			
26. **Independence:** Work for or by myself; decide for myself what kind of work I'll do and how I'll do it.			
27. **Location:** Have work that allows me to live in a town or geographic area that matches my lifestyle and allows me to do things I enjoy.			
28. **Physical challenge:** Have a job whose physical demands are challenging and rewarding.			
29. **Time freedom:** Have a flexible work schedule that allows me to have control of my time.			
30. **Beauty:** Have a job that allows me to enjoy beauty or that involves sensitivity to or for beauty.			

(continued)

(continued)

Value	Not Important	Important	Very Important
31. **Recognition:** Be recognized for the quality of my work in some visible or public way.			
32. **Moral fulfillment:** Feel that my work is contributing to a set of moral standards that I feel are very important.			
33. **Community:** Live in a town or city where I can get involved in community affairs.			

Other Values or Preferences: Write other work values or preferences that are very important to you and that you want to include in your career planning.

_____

_____

_____

_____

_____

Rank Your Most Important Values

Next, use the following worksheet to rank the top values that you would like to include in your ideal career.

YOUR MOST IMPORTANT VALUES

Look over the checklist you just completed. Select the five values you would *most* like to include in your career or job and list them below. List them in order of importance to you, beginning with the most important value. These are the values you should consider most when selecting a career or making other important life decisions.

1. _____

2. _____

3. _____

4. _____

5. _____

Key Points: Chapter 4

- Including your personal values in your ideal career will give you the most satisfaction and success.

- Work values are motivators that make you feel your work has meaning or that can cause you to feel good about your work at the end of the day.

- Keep your top values in mind when making your career choice and other important life decisions.

Chapter 5

Other Key Considerations When Defining Your Ideal Job

Earlier chapters focused on the first three key considerations for defining your ideal job: your skills and abilities, your interests, and your personal values.

This chapter covers the six other important factors or steps:

- Preferred earnings
- Level of responsibility
- Location
- Special knowledge
- Work environment
- Types of people you like to work with and for

Keeping these points in mind will help you pinpoint a career that will make you successful in many ways.

How Much Money Do You Want to Make—Or Are You Willing to Accept?

As you read in Chapter 1, research shows that pay is not the most important thing for most people. Even so, many people use pay rates as a primary reason for selecting one career over another.

It's easy to say that money isn't important, but it is. Earnings are particularly important for those starting out and for those with lower incomes.

If you consider the money issue now, you'll be better able to make a good decision later, when you receive a job offer and have to balance the money with other factors. For example, would you take a position that was ideal for you in many ways if the money were a bit less than you wanted?

My Acceptable Pay Range

Pay is important, but relative. You need to consider that some compromise on money is always possible. This is why you should know in advance the pay you would accept, in addition to what you would prefer. Here are a few questions to help you define your salary range:

1. If you found the perfect job in all other respects, what would be the very least pay you would be willing to accept (per hour, week, or year)?

   _____

2. What is the upper end of pay you could expect to obtain, given your credentials and other factors?

   _____

3. What sort of income would you need to pay for a desirable lifestyle (however you want to define this)?

   _____

4. How much money do you hope to make in your next job?

   _____

Many people will take less money if the job is great in other ways— or if they simply need to survive. And we all want more pay if we can get it. Realistically, your next job will probably pay somewhere between your minimum and maximum amount. Complete the following to determine a reasonable pay range for your next position.

Reasonable lower end of what you will accept on your next position:

_____

Reasonable upper end of pay you can expect on your next job:

_____

How Much Responsibility Are You Willing to Accept?

In most organizations, those who are willing to accept more responsibility are also typically paid more. With few exceptions, if you want to earn more, you will have to accept more responsibility or get more education. Higher levels of responsibility often require you to supervise others or make decisions that affect the organization. When things don't go well, people in charge are held accountable for the performance of their area of responsibility. Some people are willing to accept this responsibility, but others, understandably, would prefer not to. Decide how much responsibility you are willing to accept and write that in the next worksheet.

MY PREFERRED LEVEL OF RESPONSIBILITY

Here are some questions to help you consider how much responsibility you want or are willing to accept in your ideal job.

1. Do you like to be in charge? _____

2. Are you good at supervising others? _____

3. Do you prefer working as part of a team? _____

4. Do you prefer working by yourself or under someone else's guidance? _____

5. Are you willing to be held accountable when things go wrong?

   _____

Jot down where you see yourself in terms of accepting responsibility for others and in other ways within an organization.

_____

_____

_____

_____

Where Do You Want Your Ideal Job to Be Located—In What City or Region?

One factor to consider when choosing a career is where, geographically, you want to work. This could be as simple a decision as finding a job that allows you to live where you are now. This might be because you want to live near your relatives, like where you live and don't want to move, or want to be close to your favorite child-care center. You may or may not be willing to relocate across town or to a distant city.

There are often good reasons for wanting to stay where you now live, although certain career opportunities may be limited unless you are willing to move. For example, if you live in a small town, some jobs may exist in small numbers, if at all. If you are willing to leave, you may be able to find jobs with higher overall wages, a larger and more varied job market, or some other advantage. Some industries cluster in particular places: music in Nashville, movies in Hollywood, fashion in New York.

When you've looked at all the options, you can make a more informed decision. If you prefer to stay but are willing to move, a good strategy is to spend a substantial part of your job-search time looking locally. If you are willing to relocate, don't make the common mistake of looking for a job "anywhere." That sort of scattered approach is both inefficient and ineffective. It is preferable to narrow your job search to a few key geographic areas and concentrate your efforts there.

Keep in mind that the right job in the wrong place is not the right job. A better course of action is to define the characteristics of the place you'd like to live.

For example, suppose you would like to live near the mountains, in a mid-sized city, and in a part of the country that has mild winters but does have four seasons. That leaves out a large number of places, doesn't it? Or it may be as simple as wanting to live near your mom. As you add more criteria, there are fewer and fewer places to look, and your job search becomes more precise. The more precise you are, the more likely you will end up with what you want. One way to do this is to consider the places you have already lived. Think about what you did and did not like about them. Use a sheet of paper to list the things you did like (on the left side) and did not like (on the right). This may help you identify the things you would like to have in a new place. You should also go to your library or the Internet to research a particular location you are considering or just to learn about the options.

✏️ **PREFERRED GEOGRAPHIC LOCATION**

Go ahead and write down where you prefer your work to be located.

_____

_____

_____

_____

_____

_____

What Special Knowledge or Interests Would You Like to Use or Pursue?

You have all sorts of life experiences, training, and education that can help you succeed in a new career. Chapter 2 helped you to record this information in detail, and you might want to look over that material before responding to the questions in this section.

Perhaps you know how to fix computers, write well, build things, keep accounting records, solve problems, or cook good food. Write down the things you have learned from schooling, training, hobbies, family experiences, and other formal or informal sources. Perhaps one or more of them could make you a very special applicant in the right setting. For example, an accountant who knows a lot about fashion would be a very special candidate if he or she wants a career with an organization that sells clothing or home furnishings or has another connection to style and fashion.

Formal education, special training, and work experience are obviously important, but leisure activities, hobbies, volunteer work, family responsibilities, and other informal activities can also help define a previously overlooked job possibility.

To help you consider alternatives, use a separate sheet of paper to make a list of the major areas in which you

1. Have received formal education or training

2. Have learned to do something from prior on-the-job, hobby, or other informal experience

3. Are very interested in, but don't have much practical experience

When you have made your list, go back and select the areas that are most interesting to you. These could give you ideas for jobs you might otherwise overlook. List your top special knowledge or interest choices on the worksheet that follows, beginning with the one that is most important to you.

SPECIAL KNOWLEDGE OR INTERESTS I MIGHT USE IN MY NEXT JOB
1. _____
_____
2. _____
_____
3. _____
_____
4. _____
_____
5. _____
_____

As you fine-tune your career choice, try to include at least one or two of your special interests or areas of knowledge. For instance, if you are looking for a job as a warehouse manager but selected your hobby of making pottery as an area where you have special knowledge, can you think of a possible job combining the two? Perhaps distributing pottery supplies or managing some part of a pottery business would be more your cup of tea than managing just any sort of warehouse.

What Sort of Work Environment Do You Prefer?

Some people don't like to work in a building without windows; others don't like work that involves sitting all day. While most of us can put up with all sorts of less-than-ideal work environments, some work environment issues will bother you more than others.

Once again, defining the things you did not like about previous work and school environments is a good way to help you define what you prefer. Think of all the places you've worked or gone to school and write down the things you didn't like about those environments. Then redefine them as positives, as in the following example. When you have completed the list for each job you've had (use extra sheets if necessary), go back and select the five environmental preferences that are really important to you. Here is one example of such a worksheet to help you get started.

Job: Accountant for the Internal Revenue Service

Things I Did Not Like About the Workplace	Environment I Would Like in My Next Job
too noisy	quiet workplace
no variety in work	lots of variety in work
no windows	my own window
parking was a problem	my own airstrip (just kidding)
too much sitting	more activity
not people-oriented	more customer contact
indoors in nice weather	more outside work
too large an organization	smaller organization

Other issues to consider when defining your ideal work environment include frequent travel, work hazards, job stress, and physical demands.

✎ MY PREFERRED WORK ENVIRONMENT

Write down those things about your work environment that are most important to include in your next job on the following lines. List your most important selection first, followed by others in order of importance.

1. _____

_____

(continued)

(continued)

```
2. _____

   _____

3. _____

   _____

4. _____

   _____

5. _____

   _____
```

What Types of People Do You Prefer to Work With?

An important element in enjoying your job is the people you work with and for. If you have ever had a rotten boss or worked with a group of losers, you know exactly why this is so important. Keep in mind that what someone else defines as a good group of people to work with might not be good for you.

You could argue that there is no way to know in advance the types of people you will end up having as co-workers. However, first impressions work both ways. Your potential employer judges you within the first 30 seconds of a face-to-face meeting. You can do the same regarding your potential boss and co-workers. This is why it is a good idea to meet with the people you will work with before you accept a position. Ask them questions if you can't get a good read on the type of people they are. If you haven't already given any thought to the subject, the following exercise will help you do just that.

Think about all your past jobs (work, military, volunteer, school, and so on) and your co-workers at those jobs. Write down the things you didn't like about your co-workers and then redefine them into qualities you would like to see in your workmates. When your list is complete, go back and identify the types of people you would really like to work with in your next job. Then select the five qualities that are most important to you.

CHARACTERISTICS OF THE PEOPLE I WOULD PREFER TO WORK WITH

Write those characteristics below, in their order of importance to you.

1. _____

_____

2. _____

_____

3. _____

_____

4. _____

_____

5. _____

_____

You Have Defined Nine Ideal Career Characteristics

The activities you completed in Chapters 1 through 5 have helped you more clearly define the preferred characteristics of your next career—and we haven't reviewed job titles or industries yet! Any one of these preferred characteristics, if left unresolved, can cause you problems during your search for a job. Even worse, pursuing a career that is in major conflict with one or more of these factors can lead to job failure or unhappiness.

So spend whatever time is needed to resolve each of the nine factors so that you are clear what you would prefer in your ideal job.

Key Points: Chapter 5

- Although money may not be everything, when deciding your career focus, it is important to consider the money issue in advance so you can make good choices.

- Different people want different amounts of responsibility on the job.

- Keep in mind that the right job in the wrong place is not the right job. A better course of action is to define the characteristics of the place you'd like to live.

- You have all sorts of life experience, training, and education that can help you succeed in a new career. Include the experiences you enjoy the most in your definition of your ideal career.

- Your work environment plays a role in your contentment on the job.

- An important element in enjoying your job is the people you work with and for. If you have ever had a rotten boss or worked with a group of losers, you know exactly why this is so important.

Chapter 6

Finally! Identify Specific Job Titles

By now you should have a better sense of your skills, interests, work values, and other key elements of your ideal career. Keep those factors in mind as you review the job descriptions in this chapter.

This chapter is designed to give you a good idea of what sort of job you want in terms of a job title. It is the longest chapter in the book and describes more than 288 major job titles, including their education or training required, skill levels, earnings, growth, and other details to help you make a good decision. Although this chapter is long, don't worry. You won't need to read it all.

Note: *You may have expected this chapter at the beginning of the book, but saving the job titles until now is a strategy to shake you out of the conventional approach that focuses narrowly on job titles. That narrow focus causes people to overlook far more important matters for their long-term career satisfaction and success.*

Why Accurate Information About Specific Jobs Is Important

You have identified your interests and learned about other factors to consider in your career choice. But how can you identify specific jobs that would be best for you? Will they require more training or education? What do they pay? Do they offer good employment opportunities?

Accurate information about specific jobs is important for your career planning, but you have thousands of job titles to consider. Even within one interest area, there are many jobs at different levels of pay, with different levels of required training, and with very different work settings.

For example, in the health-care field you might consider being a medical doctor, an emergency medical technician, or a home health-care worker. Each of these jobs has very different entry requirements, pay, and tasks.

These differences affect your educational planning, workday, work environment, pay, lifestyle, and more. That's why accurate job descriptions can help you make good career decisions.

The jobs described in this chapter appear in a longer form in the *Occupational Outlook Handbook,* a book published every two years by the U.S. Department of Labor and available from JIST. The *OOH* is also available online at www.bls.gov/oco/home.htm. The data in the job descriptions comes from research done by the U.S. Department of Labor.

How the Job Descriptions Are Organized

Although there are many career options to consider, the following information makes the task easier. In Chapter 3, you reviewed 16 career interest areas and identified those that interested you most.

This chapter organizes job descriptions into those same 16 interest areas. Some widely used career clustering schemes assign jobs to more than one cluster, but we assign each job only to the single interest area that best describes the work done by the majority of workers.

Within each interest area, jobs are organized according to the level of education or training that is usually the minimal requirement: on-the-job training or work experience, postsecondary education or training of less than four years, or a bachelor's degree or higher. Within the job descriptions, you can find the specific level of education or training usually required (sometimes more than one).

Interest area

4. Business and Administration

Advertising Sales Agents

Sell or solicit advertising, including graphic art, advertising space in publications, custom-made signs, or TV and radio advertising time. **Skill levels:** *High:* Artistic, interpersonal. *Medium:* Communication, managerial, mathematics. *Low:* Mechanical, science. **Education and training:** Moderate-term on-the-job training. **Annual earnings:** $43,360. **Annual openings:** 4,510. **Job growth through 2018:** 7.2%.

Job description

Review Job Titles

Refer to Chapter 3 to recall your top interest areas. Highlight or circle your top interest areas in the pages that follow.

Then skim the job titles listed under your top interest areas. Checkmark the jobs that sound most interesting to you. When you checkmark a job, also look closely at the jobs at a similar level of education or training to identify other possible job options. Continue with your other top interest areas and checkmark all the related jobs that interest you.

The job descriptions are pretty easy to understand. They begin with the formal job title, followed by a brief description of the job. The skill levels required for the job are listed. The skill information is followed by the specific minimal level(s) of education or training typically needed for entry to the job, annual earnings for those working in the job, projected number of job openings per year, and projected job growth through 2018. Note that earnings are "median" earnings, where half of all workers in that job earn less and half more. New or less-experienced workers typically earn less.

> **Note:** *Don't read every job description at this time. Just check the ones that interest you. Checkmark jobs that interest you even if you don't have the education for that job or if there is some other barrier. Later, you will be asked to read your checked jobs more carefully and select those that most interest you. For now, simply check the jobs that are even somewhat interesting to you.*

Don't Overlook the End of This Chapter

The end of this chapter has additional information on the job descriptions and includes an exercise to help you narrow down your choices.

1. Agriculture and Natural Resources

Education/Training Usually Required: On-the-Job Training or Work Experience

Agricultural Inspectors

Inspect agricultural commodities, processing equipment and facilities, and fish and logging operations to ensure compliance with regulations and laws governing health, quality, and safety. **Skill levels:** *High:* Science. *Medium:* Communication, interpersonal, managerial, mathematics, mechanical. *Low:* Artistic. **Education and training:** Work experience in a related occupation. **Annual earnings:** $41,500. **Annual openings:** 550. **Job growth through 2018:** 12.8%.

Agricultural Workers, Other

Working mostly on farms or ranches, but also in nurseries and slaughterhouses, raise crop plants, animals, and other agricultural products and bring them to market. **Skill levels:** *High:* Managerial, mechanical, science. *Medium:* Communication, interpersonal, mathematics. *Low:* Artistic. **Education and training:** Work experience in a related occupation. **Annual earnings:** $19,510. **Annual openings:** 480. **Job growth through 2018:** 5.8%.

Animal Care and Service Workers

Train, feed, water, groom, bathe, and exercise animals and clean, disinfect, and repair their cages. **Skill levels:** *Medium:* Managerial, mechanical, science. *Low:* Communication, interpersonal, mathematics. **Education and training:** Short-term on-the-job training; moderate-term on-the-job training. **Annual earnings:** $20,070. **Annual openings:** 9,260. **Job growth through 2018:** 20.6%.

Farmers, Ranchers, and Agricultural Managers

Direct activities on farms and other agricultural establishments. **Skill levels:** *High:* Managerial, mathematics, mechanical, science. *Medium:* Interpersonal. *Low:* Artistic, communication. **Education and training:** Long-term on-the-job training; work experience plus degree. **Annual earnings:** $55,712. **Annual openings:** 12,520. **Job growth through 2018:** −5.2%.

Fishers and Fishing Vessel Operators

Catch and trap various types of marine life for human consumption, animal feed, bait, and other uses. **Skill levels:** *High:* Mechanical. *Medium:* Managerial, science. *Low:* Mathematics. **Education and training:** Moderate-term on-the-job training. **Annual earnings:** $23,600. **Annual openings:** 920. **Job growth through 2018:** −7.7%.

Floral Designers

Design, cut, and arrange live, dried, or artificial flowers and foliage. **Skill levels:** *High:* Artistic, managerial. *Low:* Interpersonal, mathematics, mechanical. **Education and training:** Short-term on-the-job training. **Annual earnings:** $23,530. **Annual openings:** 2,340. **Job growth through 2018:** −2.5%.

Food Processing Occupations

Process raw food products into the finished goods sold by grocers, wholesalers, restaurants, or institutional food services. **Skill levels:** *Medium:* Mechanical. *Low:* Artistic, managerial, science. **Education and training:** Short-term on-the-job training; moderate-term on-the-job training; long-term on-the-job training. **Annual earnings:** $24,351. **Annual openings:** 23,420. **Job growth through 2018:** 3.9%.

Forest and Conservation Workers

Under supervision, perform manual labor necessary to develop, maintain, or protect forests, forested areas, and woodlands through such activities as raising and transporting tree seedlings; combating insects, pests, and diseases harmful to trees; and building erosion and water control structures. **Skill levels:** *High:* Interpersonal, managerial, mathematics, mechanical, science. *Medium:* Communication. *Low:* Artistic. **Education and training:** Moderate-term on-the-job training. **Annual earnings:** $25,580. **Annual openings:** 450. **Job growth through 2018:** 8.5%.

Graders and Sorters, Agricultural Products

Grade, sort, or classify unprocessed food and other agricultural products by size, weight, color, or condition. **Skill levels:** *Low:* Artistic, science. **Education and training:** Work experience in a related occupation. **Annual earnings:** $19,010. **Annual openings:** 690. **Job growth through 2018:** 0.2%.

Grounds Maintenance Workers

Perform a variety of tasks necessary to achieve a pleasant and functional outdoor environment. **Skill levels:** *High:* Mechanical. *Medium:* Artistic. *Low:* Managerial, science. **Education and training:** Short-term on-the-job training; moderate-term on-the-job training; work experience in a related occupation. **Annual earnings:** $25,623. **Annual openings:** 44,950. **Job growth through 2018:** 17.7%.

Hazardous Materials Removal Workers

Identify, remove, pack, transport, or dispose of hazardous materials, including asbestos, lead-based paint, waste oil, fuel, transmission fluid, radioactive materials, contaminated soil, and others. **Skill levels:** *High:* Mechanical, science. *Low:* Mathematics. **Education and training:** Moderate-term on-the-job training. **Annual earnings:** $37,280. **Annual openings:** 1,780. **Job growth through 2018:** 14.8%.

Logging Workers

Harvest forest trees for the timber that provides the raw material for consumer and industrial products. **Skill levels:** *High:* Mechanical. *Low:* Managerial, science. **Education and training:** Moderate-term on-the-job training. **Annual earnings:** $32,335. **Annual openings:** 2,210. **Job growth through 2018:** 5.9%.

Pest Control Workers

Spray or release chemical solutions or toxic gases and set traps to kill pests and vermin, such as mice, termites, and roaches, that infest buildings and surrounding areas. **Skill levels:** *High:* Interpersonal. *Medium:* Managerial, mathematics, mechanical, science. *Low:* Artistic, communication. **Education and training:** Moderate-term on-the-job training. **Annual earnings:** $30,410. **Annual openings:** 3,400. **Job growth through 2018:** 15.3%.

Water and Liquid Waste Treatment Plant and System Operators

Operate or control an entire process or system of machines, often through the use of control boards, to transfer or treat water or liquid waste. **Skill levels:** *High:* Mathematics, mechanical, science. *Medium:* Managerial. *Low:* Artistic, communication. **Education and training:** Long-term on-the-job training. **Annual earnings:** $39,850. **Annual openings:** 4,690. **Job growth through 2018:** 19.8%.

Education/Training Usually Required: Postsecondary, Less Than Four Years

No occupations at this level.

Education/Training Usually Required: Bachelor's Degree or Higher

Agricultural and Food Scientists

Study farm crops, animals, and food products to develop ways of improving their quantity and quality. **Skill levels:** *High:* Communication, managerial, mathematics, science. *Medium:* Artistic, interpersonal, mechanical. **Education and training:** Bachelor's degree; doctoral degree. **Annual earnings:** $59,180. **Annual openings:** 1,570. **Job growth through 2018:** 15.6%.

Conservation Scientists and Foresters

Manage the use and development of forests, rangelands, and other natural resources. **Skill levels:** *High:* Communication, interpersonal, managerial, mathematics, science. *Medium:* Artistic, mechanical. **Education and training:** Bachelor's degree. **Annual earnings:** $57,769. **Annual openings:** 670. **Job growth through 2018:** 12.0%.

Environmental Scientists and Specialists

Use knowledge of the natural sciences to protect the environment by identifying problems and finding solutions that minimize hazards to the health of the environment and the population. **Skill levels:** *High:* Communication, mathematics, science. *Medium:* Artistic, managerial. *Low:* Interpersonal. **Education and training:** Master's degree. **Annual earnings:** $61,010. **Annual openings:** 4,840. **Job growth through 2018:** 27.9%.

Farmers, Ranchers, and Agricultural Managers

Direct activities on farms and other agricultural establishments. **Skill levels:** *High:* Managerial, mathematics, mechanical, science. *Medium:* Interpersonal. *Low:* Artistic, communication. **Education and training:** Long-term on-the-job training; work experience plus degree. **Annual earnings:** $55,712. **Annual openings:** 12,520. **Job growth through 2018:** –5.2%.

2. Architecture and Construction

Education/Training Usually Required: On-the-Job Training or Work Experience

Boilermakers

Construct, assemble, maintain, and repair stationary steam boilers and boiler house auxiliaries. **Skill levels:** *High:* Mathematics, mechanical. *Medium:* Communication, managerial, science. *Low:* Interpersonal. **Education and training:** Long-term on-the-job training. **Annual earnings:** $56,100. **Annual openings:** 810. **Job growth through 2018:** 18.8%.

Brickmasons, Blockmasons, and Stonemasons

Create attractive, durable surfaces and structures, using bricks, concrete blocks, and natural stone. **Skill levels:** *High:* Mathematics. *Medium:* Artistic, mechanical, science. *Low:* Interpersonal, managerial. **Education and training:** Long-term on-the-job training. **Annual earnings:** $45,363. **Annual openings:** 5,900. **Job growth through 2018:** 11.5%.

Carpenters

Build, install, and repair structures and fixtures made from wood and other materials. **Skill levels:** *High:* Managerial, mathematics, mechanical. *Medium:* Artistic, science. *Low:* Communication, interpersonal. **Education and training:** Long-term on-the-job training. **Annual earnings:** $39,470. **Annual openings:** 32,540. **Job growth through 2018:** 12.9%.

Carpet, Floor, and Tile Installers and Finishers

Lay floor coverings in homes, offices, hospitals, stores, restaurants, and other types of buildings; install tiles on floors, walls, and ceilings. **Skill levels:** *High:* Mathematics. *Medium:* Artistic, managerial, mechanical. *Low:* Interpersonal, science. **Education and training:** Moderate-term on-the-job training; long-term on-the-job training. **Annual earnings:** $37,620. **Annual openings:** 5,410. **Job growth through 2018:** 7.1%.

Cement Masons, Concrete Finishers, Segmental Pavers, and Terrazzo Workers

Work with concrete to create various kinds of structures. **Skill levels:** *High:* Mathematics. *Medium:* Mechanical. *Low:* Artistic, interpersonal, science. **Education and training:** Moderate-term on-the-job training; long-term on-the-job training. **Annual earnings:** $35,463. **Annual openings:** 7,900. **Job growth through 2018:** 12.8%.

Coin, Vending, and Amusement Machine Servicers and Repairers

Install, service, adjust, or repair coin, vending, or amusement machines, including video games, jukeboxes, pinball machines, and slot machines. **Skill levels:** *Medium:* Mechanical. **Education and training:** Moderate-term on-the-job training. **Annual earnings:** $30,460. **Annual openings:** 1,770. **Job growth through 2018:** 7.0%.

Construction and Building Inspectors

Inspect structures, using engineering skills to determine structural soundness and compliance with specifications, building codes, and other regulations. **Skill levels:** *Low:* Artistic, interpersonal, mathematics. **Education and training:** Work experience in a related occupation. **Annual earnings:** $51,530. **Annual openings:** 3,970. **Job growth through 2018:** 16.8%.

Construction Equipment Operators

Use machinery to move construction materials, earth, and other heavy materials at construction sites and mines. **Skill levels:** *High:* Mechanical. *Medium:* Managerial, mathematics, science. **Education and training:** Moderate-term on-the-job training. **Annual earnings:** $39,098. **Annual openings:** 13,640. **Job growth through 2018:** 12.0%.

Construction Laborers

Perform tasks involving physical labor at building, highway, and heavy construction projects; tunnel and shaft excavations; and demolition sites. **Skill levels:** *Medium:* Mechanical. *Low:* Mathematics, science. **Education and training:** Moderate-term on-the-job training. **Annual earnings:** $29,150. **Annual openings:** 33,940. **Job growth through 2018:** 20.5%.

Drywall and Ceiling Tile Installers, Tapers, Plasterers, and Stucco Masons

Build, apply, or fasten interior and exterior wallboards or wall coverings in residential, commercial, and other structures. **Skill levels:** *High:* Managerial, mathematics, mechanical, science. *Medium:* Artistic, interpersonal. *Low:* Communication. **Education and training:** Moderate-term on-the-job training; long-term on-the-job training. **Annual earnings:** $38,398. **Annual openings:** 5,730. **Job growth through 2018:** 12.0%.

Electricians

Install and maintain the wiring, fuses, and other components through which electricity flows. **Skill levels:** *High:* Mechanical. *Medium:* Managerial, mathematics. *Low:* Artistic, interpersonal. **Education and training:** Long-term on-the-job training. **Annual earnings:** $47,180. **Annual openings:** 25,090. **Job growth through 2018:** 11.9%.

Glaziers

Select, cut, install, replace, and remove all types of glass. **Skill levels:** *Medium:* Mathematics, mechanical. *Low:* Science. **Education and training:** Long-term on-the-job training. **Annual earnings:** $35,590. **Annual openings:** 2,390. **Job growth through 2018:** 7.7%.

Home Appliance Repairers

Repair, adjust, or install all types of electric or gas household appliances, such as refrigerators, washers, dryers, and ovens. **Skill levels:** *High:* Mechanical, science. *Medium:* Interpersonal, managerial. *Low:* Communication, mathematics. **Education and training:** Long-term on-the-job training. **Annual earnings:** $34,200. **Annual openings:** 870. **Job growth through 2018:** 2.2%.

Insulation Workers

Install the materials used to insulate buildings and equipment. **Skill levels:** *Medium:* Mathematics, mechanical, science. *Low:* Artistic, interpersonal, managerial. **Education and training:** Moderate-term on-the-job training. **Annual earnings:** $34,920. **Annual openings:** 2,870. **Job growth through 2018:** 17.4%.

Line Installers and Repairers

Install and maintain the wires and cables that provide customers with electrical power and services for voice, video, and data communications. **Skill levels:** *High:* Mechanical. *Medium:* Managerial, mathematics, science. *Low:* Artistic, communication, interpersonal. **Education and training:** Long-term on-the-job training. **Annual earnings:** $52,146. **Annual openings:** 7,340. **Job growth through 2018:** 2.3%.

Maintenance and Repair Workers, General

Perform work involving the skills of two or more maintenance or craft occupations to keep machines, mechanical equipment, or the structure of an establishment in repair. **Skill levels:** *High:* Mechanical. *Medium:* Science. *Low:* Artistic, interpersonal, managerial, mathematics. **Education and training:** Moderate-term on-the-job training. **Annual earnings:** $34,620. **Annual openings:** 35,750. **Job growth through 2018:** 10.9%.

Painters and Paperhangers

Apply paint and indoor wall coverings to make surfaces clean, attractive, and vibrant and protect exterior surfaces from erosion caused by exposure to the weather. **Skill levels:** *Medium:* Artistic, managerial, mathematics, mechanical. *Low:* Science. **Education and training:** Moderate-term on-the-job training. **Annual earnings:** $33,807. **Annual openings:** 10,660. **Job growth through 2018:** 6.6%.

Plumbers, Pipelayers, Pipefitters, and Steamfitters

Install, maintain, and repair many different types of pipe systems. **Skill levels:** *High:* Mechanical. *Low:* Artistic, interpersonal, managerial, mathematics, science. **Education and training:** Short-term on-the-job training; long-term on-the-job training. **Annual earnings:** $44,922. **Annual openings:** 19,830. **Job growth through 2018:** 15.5%.

Roofers

Cover roofs of structures with shingles, slate, asphalt, aluminum, wood, and related materials. **Skill levels:** *High:* Mathematics, mechanical. *Medium:* Interpersonal, managerial, science. **Education and training:** Moderate-term on-the-job training. **Annual earnings:** $33,970. **Annual openings:** 3,010. **Job growth through 2018:** 3.8%.

Structural and Reinforcing Iron and Metal Workers

Place and install iron or steel girders, columns, and other construction materials to form buildings, bridges, and other structures. **Skill levels:** *High:* Managerial, mathematics, mechanical. *Low:* Artistic, communication, interpersonal, science. **Education and training:** Long-term on-the-job training. **Annual earnings:** $43,135. **Annual openings:** 2,820. **Job growth through 2018:** 12.4%.

Surveyors, Cartographers, Photogrammetrists, and Surveying and Mapping Technicians

Measure and map the Earth's surface. **Skill levels:** *Medium:* Artistic, mathematics, mechanical. *Low:* Communication, managerial, science. **Education and training:**

Moderate-term on-the-job training; bachelor's degree. **Annual earnings:** $45,522. **Annual openings:** 5,910. **Job growth through 2018:** 18.8%.

Education/Training Usually Required: Postsecondary, Less Than Four Years

Drafters

Prepare technical drawings and plans, which are used to build everything from manufactured products such as toys, toasters, industrial machinery, and spacecraft to structures such as houses, office buildings, and oil and gas pipelines. **Skill levels:** *High:* Artistic, mathematics. *Medium:* Communication, interpersonal, science. *Low:* Managerial, mechanical. **Education and training:** Postsecondary vocational training. **Annual earnings:** $47,150. **Annual openings:** 6,570. **Job growth through 2018:** 4.2%.

Heating, Air-Conditioning, and Refrigeration Mechanics and Installers

Set up or repair heating, central air conditioning, or refrigeration systems. **Skill levels:** *High:* Mathematics, mechanical, science. *Medium:* Communication, interpersonal, managerial. *Low:* Artistic. **Education and training:** Postsecondary vocational training. **Annual earnings:** $41,100. **Annual openings:** 13,620. **Job growth through 2018:** 28.1%.

Education/Training Usually Required: Bachelor's Degree or Higher

Architects, Except Landscape and Naval

Plan and design structures such as private residences, office buildings, theaters, factories, and other structural property. **Skill levels:** *High:* Artistic, communication, interpersonal, managerial, mathematics, science. *Low:* Mechanical. **Education and training:** Bachelor's degree. **Annual earnings:** $72,700. **Annual openings:** 4,680. **Job growth through 2018:** 16.2%.

Construction Managers

Plan, direct, and coordinate construction projects. **Skill levels:** *High:* Managerial. *Medium:* Interpersonal, mathematics. *Low:* Artistic, communication. **Education and training:** Bachelor's degree. **Annual earnings:** $82,330. **Annual openings:** 13,770. **Job growth through 2018:** 17.2%.

Cost Estimators

Prepare cost estimates for product manufacturing, construction projects, or services to aid management in bidding on or determining price of product or service. **Skill levels:** *Medium:* Managerial, mathematics. *Low:* Communication, interpersonal. **Education and training:** Bachelor's degree. **Annual earnings:** $57,300. **Annual openings:** 10,360. **Job growth through 2018:** 25.3%.

Landscape Architects

Plan and design land areas for such projects as parks and other recreational facilities; airports; highways; hospitals; schools; land subdivisions; and commercial, industrial, and residential sites. **Skill levels:** *High:* Artistic, communication, interpersonal, managerial, mathematics, science. *Low:* Mechanical. **Education and training:** Bachelor's degree. **Annual earnings:** $60,560. **Annual openings:** 980. **Job growth through 2018:** 19.7%.

Surveyors, Cartographers, Photogrammetrists, and Surveying and Mapping Technicians

Measure and map the Earth's surface. **Skill levels:** *Medium:* Artistic, mathematics, mechanical. *Low:* Communication, managerial, science. **Education and training:** Moderate-term on-the-job training; bachelor's degree. **Annual earnings:** $45,522. **Annual openings:** 5,910. **Job growth through 2018:** 18.8%.

3. Arts and Communication

Education/Training Usually Required: On-the-Job Training or Work Experience

Actors, Producers, and Directors

Express ideas and create images in theater, film, radio, television, and other performing arts media, interpreting a writer's script to entertain, inform, or instruct an audience. **Skill levels:** *High:* Artistic, communication, interpersonal, managerial. *Low:* Mechanical, science. **Education and training:** Long-term on-the-job training; work experience plus degree. **Annual earnings:** $66,720. **Annual openings:** 6,120. **Job growth through 2018:** 10.9%.

Announcers

Perform a variety of speaking tasks on radio or TV, including giving information, interviewing, and providing commentary; off the air, may prepare scripts or operate station equipment. **Skill levels:** *High:* Artistic, communication, interpersonal. *Medium:* Managerial, mechanical. *Low:* Mathematics, science. **Education and training:** Moderate-term on-the-job training; long-term on-the-job training. **Annual earnings:** $27,467. **Annual openings:** 2,000. **Job growth through 2018:** –3.5%.

Artists and Related Workers

Use a variety of methods—painting, sculpting, or illustration—and an assortment of materials to communicate ideas, thoughts, or feelings. **Skill levels:** *High:* Artistic, communication. *Medium:* Interpersonal, managerial, mathematics, mechanical, science. **Education and training:** Long-term on-the-job training; bachelor's degree; work experience plus degree. **Annual earnings:** $62,101. **Annual openings:** 7,550. **Job growth through 2018:** 11.6%.

Bookbinders and Bindery Workers

Produce books and other printed materials by setting up or operating binding machines or by performing highly skilled hand-finishing operations. **Skill levels:**

High: Mechanical. *Low:* Artistic, managerial, mathematics, science. **Education and training:** Short-term on-the-job training; moderate-term on-the-job training. **Annual earnings:** $28,450. **Annual openings:** 970. **Job growth through 2018:** −19.4%.

Broadcast and Sound Engineering Technicians and Radio Operators

Perform a wide variety of tasks to set up, maintain, and operate electrical equipment used in radio and television broadcasts, concerts, plays, sound recordings, and movies. **Skill levels:** *High:* Mechanical. *Medium:* Artistic, communication, managerial, science. *Low:* Interpersonal, mathematics. **Education and training:** Moderate-term on-the-job training; postsecondary vocational training; associate degree. **Annual earnings:** $38,298. **Annual openings:** 4,360. **Job growth through 2018:** 7.8%.

Communications Equipment Operators

Relay incoming, outgoing, and interoffice calls or assist customers with clerical duties such as offering directory information, taking messages, greeting and announcing visitors, or, in some cases, handling billing requests or emergency calls. **Skill levels:** *Low:* Communication. **Education and training:** Short-term on-the-job training. **Annual earnings:** $25,766. **Annual openings:** 3,680. **Job growth through 2018:** −10.0%.

Dancers and Choreographers

Perform dances or create and teach dance. **Skill levels:** *High:* Artistic, interpersonal, managerial. *Low:* Communication. **Education and training:** Long-term on-the-job training; work experience in a related occupation. **Annual earnings:** $37,860. **Annual openings:** 1,520. **Job growth through 2018:** 6.0%.

Musicians, Singers, and Related Workers

Play musical instruments, sing, compose or arrange music, or conduct groups in instrumental or vocal performances. **Skill levels:** *High:* Artistic. *Medium:* Interpersonal, mechanical. *Low:* Communication, managerial, science. **Education and training:** Long-term on-the-job training; work experience plus degree. **Annual earnings:** $45,090. **Annual openings:** 6,810. **Job growth through 2018:** 8.2%.

Photographers

Photograph persons, subjects, merchandise, or other commercial products. **Skill levels:** *High:* Artistic, mechanical. *Medium:* Interpersonal, managerial, science. *Low:* Communication, mathematics. **Education and training:** Long-term on-the-job training. **Annual earnings:** $29,770. **Annual openings:** 4,800. **Job growth through 2018:** 11.5%.

Photographic Process Workers and Processing Machine Operators

Use various machines to create prints from film or digital photographs. **Skill levels:** *Medium:* Artistic, mechanical, science. *Low:* Managerial, mathematics. **Education and training:** Short-term on-the-job training. **Annual earnings:** $21,946. **Annual openings:** 1,860. **Job growth through 2018:** −16.1%.

Prepress Technicians and Workers

Set up and prepare material for printing presses. **Skill levels:** *High:* Mechanical. *Medium:* Artistic, managerial. *Low:* Communication, interpersonal, mathematics, science. **Education and training:** Long-term on-the-job training; postsecondary vocational training. **Annual earnings:** $35,232. **Annual openings:** 940. **Job growth through 2018:** –13.4%.

Printing Machine Operators

Set up or operate various types of printing machines, such as offset, letterset, intaglio, or gravure presses, or screen printers to produce print on paper or other materials. **Skill levels:** *High:* Mechanical. *Medium:* Mathematics, science. *Low:* Artistic. **Education and training:** Moderate-term on-the-job training. **Annual earnings:** $32,970. **Annual openings:** 4,100. **Job growth through 2018:** –5.5%.

Education/Training Usually Required: Postsecondary, Less Than Four Years

Broadcast and Sound Engineering Technicians and Radio Operators

Perform a wide variety of tasks to set up, maintain, and operate electrical equipment used in radio and television broadcasts, concerts, plays, sound recordings, and movies. **Skill levels:** *High:* Mechanical. *Medium:* Artistic, communication, managerial, science. *Low:* Interpersonal, mathematics. **Education and training:** Moderate-term on-the-job training; postsecondary vocational training; associate degree. **Annual earnings:** $38,298. **Annual openings:** 4,360. **Job growth through 2018:** 7.8%.

Electronic Home Entertainment Equipment Installers and Repairers

Repair, adjust, or install audio or television receivers, stereo systems, camcorders, video systems, or other electronic home entertainment equipment. **Skill levels:** *High:* Mechanical, science. *Medium:* Mathematics. *Low:* Artistic, communication, interpersonal, managerial. **Education and training:** Postsecondary vocational training. **Annual earnings:** $32,320. **Annual openings:** 1,430. **Job growth through 2018:** 10.8%.

Fashion Designers

Design clothing and accessories. **Skill levels:** *High:* Artistic, interpersonal, managerial, mathematics, science. *Medium:* Communication, mechanical. **Education and training:** Associate degree. **Annual earnings:** $64,260. **Annual openings:** 720. **Job growth through 2018:** 0.8%.

Gaming Services Occupations

Perform various duties in casinos, state lottery operations, racetracks, and charitable gaming operations. **Skill levels:** *High:* Artistic. *Medium:* Communication, mechanical. *Low:* Interpersonal, managerial, mathematics. **Education and training:** Postsecondary vocational training. **Annual earnings:** $36,470. **Annual openings:** 440. **Job growth through 2018:** –22.6%.

Interior Designers

Plan, design, and furnish interiors of residential, commercial, or industrial buildings. **Skill levels:** *High:* Artistic, interpersonal, mathematics. *Medium:* Communication, managerial, mechanical, science. **Education and training:** Associate degree. **Annual earnings:** $46,180. **Annual openings:** 3,590. **Job growth through 2018:** 19.4%.

Prepress Technicians and Workers

Set up and prepare material for printing presses. **Skill levels:** *High:* Mechanical. *Medium:* Artistic, managerial. *Low:* Communication, interpersonal, mathematics, science. **Education and training:** Long-term on-the-job training; postsecondary vocational training. **Annual earnings:** $35,232. **Annual openings:** 940. **Job growth through 2018:** –13.4%.

Radio and Telecommunications Equipment Installers and Repairers

Set up and maintain a variety of equipment to transmit communications signals and connect to the Internet. **Skill levels:** *High:* Mechanical, science. *Medium:* Interpersonal, managerial, mathematics. *Low:* Artistic, communication. **Education and training:** Postsecondary vocational training. **Annual earnings:** $55,138. **Annual openings:** 3,660. **Job growth through 2018:** –0.3%.

Education/Training Usually Required: Bachelor's Degree or Higher

Actors, Producers, and Directors

Express ideas and create images in theater, film, radio, television, and other performing arts media, interpreting a writer's script to entertain, inform, or instruct an audience. **Skill levels:** *High:* Artistic, communication, interpersonal, managerial. *Low:* Mechanical, science. **Education and training:** Long-term on-the-job training; work experience plus degree. **Annual earnings:** $66,720. **Annual openings:** 6,120. **Job growth through 2018:** 10.9%.

Artists and Related Workers

Use a variety of methods—painting, sculpting, or illustration—and an assortment of materials to communicate ideas, thoughts, or feelings. **Skill levels:** *High:* Artistic, communication. *Medium:* Interpersonal, managerial, mathematics, mechanical, science. **Education and training:** Long-term on-the-job training; bachelor's degree; work experience plus degree. **Annual earnings:** $62,101. **Annual openings:** 7,550. **Job growth through 2018:** 11.6%.

Authors, Writers, and Editors

Develop a wide variety of written materials for books, magazines, online publications, newsletters, advertisements, and other media. **Skill levels:** *High:* Artistic, communication. *Medium:* Interpersonal, managerial. *Low:* Mechanical, science. **Education and training:** Bachelor's degree. **Annual earnings:** $51,706. **Annual openings:** 8,810. **Job growth through 2018:** 7.8%.

Commercial and Industrial Designers

Develop and design manufactured products, such as cars, home appliances, and children's toys. **Skill levels:** *High:* Artistic, mathematics. *Medium:* Communication, interpersonal, mechanical, science. *Low:* Managerial. **Education and training:** Bachelor's degree. **Annual earnings:** $58,060. **Annual openings:** 1,760. **Job growth through 2018:** 9.0%.

Graphic Designers

Design or create graphics to meet specific commercial or promotional needs, such as packaging, displays, or logos. **Skill levels:** *High:* Artistic. **Education and training:** Bachelor's degree. **Annual earnings:** $43,180. **Annual openings:** 12,480. **Job growth through 2018:** 12.9%.

Musicians, Singers, and Related Workers

Play musical instruments, sing, compose or arrange music, or conduct groups in instrumental or vocal performances. **Skill levels:** *High:* Artistic. *Medium:* Interpersonal, mechanical. *Low:* Communication, managerial, science. **Education and training:** Long-term on-the-job training; work experience plus degree. **Annual earnings:** $45,090. **Annual openings:** 6,810. **Job growth through 2018:** 8.2%.

News Analysts, Reporters, and Correspondents

Gather information, prepare stories, and make broadcasts that inform the public about local, state, national, and international events; present points of view on current issues; and report on the actions of public officials, corporate executives, interest groups, and others who exercise power. **Skill levels:** *High:* Artistic, communication. *Medium:* Interpersonal. *Low:* Managerial, mathematics, science. **Education and training:** Bachelor's degree. **Annual earnings:** $36,157. **Annual openings:** 1,930. **Job growth through 2018:** –6.3%.

Public Relations Specialists

Engage in promoting or creating good will for individuals, groups, or organizations by writing or selecting favorable publicity material and releasing it through various communications media. **Skill levels:** *High:* Artistic, communication, interpersonal. *Medium:* Managerial. **Education and training:** Bachelor's degree. **Annual earnings:** $51,960. **Annual openings:** 13,130. **Job growth through 2018:** 24.0%.

Technical Writers

Write technical materials, such as equipment manuals, appendices, or operating and maintenance instructions. **Skill levels:** *High:* Artistic, communication. *Medium:* Interpersonal, science. *Low:* Managerial, mechanical. **Education and training:** Bachelor's degree. **Annual earnings:** $62,730. **Annual openings:** 1,680. **Job growth through 2018:** 18.2%.

Television, Video, and Motion Picture Camera Operators and Editors

Produce video images and soundtracks that tell a story, inform or entertain an audience, or record an event. **Skill levels:** *High:* Artistic. *Medium:* Interpersonal, mechanical. *Low:* Communication, managerial, science. **Education and training:** Bachelor's degree. **Annual earnings:** $46,866. **Annual openings:** 1,820. **Job growth through 2018:** 10.5%.

4. Business and Administration

Education/Training Usually Required: On-the-Job Training or Work Experience

Advertising Sales Agents

Sell or solicit advertising, including graphic art, advertising space in publications, custom-made signs, or TV and radio advertising time. **Skill levels:** *High:* Artistic, interpersonal. *Medium:* Communication, managerial, mathematics. *Low:* Mechanical, science. **Education and training:** Moderate-term on-the-job training. **Annual earnings:** $43,360. **Annual openings:** 4,510. **Job growth through 2018:** 7.2%.

Billing and Posting Clerks and Machine Operators

Compile, compute, and record billing, accounting, statistical, and other numerical data for billing purposes. **Skill levels:** *Medium:* Communication. *Low:* Mathematics, mechanical. **Education and training:** Short-term on-the-job training. **Annual earnings:** $31,720. **Annual openings:** 16,760. **Job growth through 2018:** 15.3%.

Bookkeeping, Accounting, and Auditing Clerks

Compute, classify, and record numerical data to keep financial records complete. **Skill levels:** *Medium:* Managerial, mathematics. *Low:* Communication, interpersonal, mechanical, science. **Education and training:** Moderate-term on-the-job training. **Annual earnings:** $33,450. **Annual openings:** 46,040. **Job growth through 2018:** 10.3%.

Brokerage Clerks

Perform clerical duties involving the purchase or sale of securities. **Skill levels:** *Medium:* Communication, mathematics. *Low:* Mechanical, science. **Education and training:** Moderate-term on-the-job training. **Annual earnings:** $40,180. **Annual openings:** 1,920. **Job growth through 2018:** –2.6%.

Cargo and Freight Agents

Help transportation companies manage incoming and outgoing shipments in airline, train, or trucking terminals or on shipping docks. **Skill levels:** *Medium:* Interpersonal. *Low:* Communication, mathematics. **Education and training:** Moderate-term on-the-job training. **Annual earnings:** $36,960. **Annual openings:** 4,030. **Job growth through 2018:** 23.9%.

Couriers and Messengers

Pick up and carry messages, documents, packages, and other items between offices or departments within an establishment or to other business concerns, traveling by foot, bicycle, motorcycle, automobile, or public conveyance. **Skill levels:** *Medium:*

Mechanical. **Education and training:** Short-term on-the-job training. **Annual earnings:** $23,770. **Annual openings:** 2,810. **Job growth through 2018:** –0.3%.

Customer Service Representatives

Interact with customers to provide information in response to inquiries about products and services and to handle and resolve complaints. **Skill levels:** *Medium:* Communication, interpersonal, mechanical. *Low:* Artistic, managerial, mathematics. **Education and training:** Moderate-term on-the-job training. **Annual earnings:** $30,290. **Annual openings:** 110,840. **Job growth through 2018:** 17.7%.

Data Entry and Information Processing Workers

Enter data into a computer, operate a variety of office machines, and perform other clerical or administrative duties. **Skill levels:** *Low:* Communication, interpersonal, mechanical. **Education and training:** Moderate-term on-the-job training. **Annual earnings:** $28,837. **Annual openings:** 7,020. **Job growth through 2018:** –6.0%.

Desktop Publishers

Format typescript and graphic elements, using computer software to produce publication-ready material. **Skill levels:** *Medium:* Communication. *Low:* Mathematics, mechanical. **Education and training:** Short-term on-the-job training. **Annual earnings:** $31,720. **Annual openings:** 16,760. **Job growth through 2018:** 15.3%.

Dispatchers, Except Police, Fire, and Ambulance

Schedule and dispatch workers, work crews, equipment, or service vehicles for conveyance of materials, freight, or passengers or for normal installation, service, or emergency repairs rendered outside the place of business. **Skill levels:** *Medium:* Managerial, mechanical. *Low:* Communication, interpersonal, mathematics, science. **Education and training:** Moderate-term on-the-job training. **Annual earnings:** $34,480. **Annual openings:** 4,030. **Job growth through 2018:** –2.6%.

File Clerks

File correspondence, cards, invoices, receipts, and other records in alphabetical or numerical order or according to the filing system used. **Skill levels:** *Low:* Mathematics, mechanical. **Education and training:** Short-term on-the-job training. **Annual earnings:** $24,730. **Annual openings:** 5,160. **Job growth through 2018:** –23.4%.

Human Resource Assistants, Except Payroll and Timekeeping

Maintain the human resource records of an organization's employees. **Skill levels:** *Medium:* Communication, mathematics. *Low:* Artistic, interpersonal, managerial. **Education and training:** Short-term on-the-job training. **Annual earnings:** $36,650. **Annual openings:** 4,810. **Job growth through 2018:** –5.7%.

Industrial Production Managers

Plan, direct, and coordinate the work activities and resources necessary for manufacturing products in accordance with specifications for cost, quality, and quantity. **Skill**

levels: *High:* Managerial. *Medium:* Interpersonal. *Low:* Artistic, communication, mathematics. **Education and training:** Work experience in a related occupation. **Annual earnings:** $85,080. **Annual openings:** 5,470. **Job growth through 2018:** –7.7%.

Interviewers, Except Eligibility and Loan

Interview persons by telephone, by mail, in person, or by other means for the purpose of completing forms, applications, or questionnaires. **Skill levels:** *Low:* Artistic, communication, interpersonal. **Education and training:** Short-term on-the-job training. **Annual earnings:** $28,660. **Annual openings:** 9,210. **Job growth through 2018:** 15.6%.

Meter Readers, Utilities

Read meter and record consumption of electricity, gas, water, or steam. **Skill levels:** *Medium:* Mechanical. *Low:* Managerial, mathematics, science. **Education and training:** Short-term on-the-job training. **Annual earnings:** $34,490. **Annual openings:** 1,250. **Job growth through 2018:** –20.0%.

Office and Administrative Support Supervisors and Managers

Plan or supervise support staff to ensure that they can work efficiently. **Skill levels:** *High:* Interpersonal, managerial. *Medium:* Communication, mathematics. *Low:* Artistic, mechanical, science. **Education and training:** Work experience in a related occupation. **Annual earnings:** $46,910. **Annual openings:** 48,900. **Job growth through 2018:** 11.0%.

Office Clerks, General

Perform duties too varied and diverse to be classified in any specific office clerical occupation, requiring limited knowledge of office management systems and procedures. **Skill levels:** *Low:* Communication, mathematics. **Education and training:** Short-term on-the-job training. **Annual earnings:** $26,140. **Annual openings:** 77,090. **Job growth through 2018:** 11.9%.

Order Clerks

Receive and process incoming orders for materials; merchandise; classified ads; or services such as repairs, installations, or rental of facilities. **Skill levels:** *Low:* Artistic, communication, interpersonal, managerial, mathematics, mechanical. **Education and training:** Short-term on-the-job training. **Annual earnings:** $28,510. **Annual openings:** 6,960. **Job growth through 2018:** –26.1%.

Payroll and Timekeeping Clerks

Compile and post employee time and payroll data. **Skill levels:** *High:* Mathematics. *Medium:* Communication. *Low:* Interpersonal, managerial, mechanical. **Education and training:** Moderate-term on-the-job training. **Annual earnings:** $36,000. **Annual openings:** 4,950. **Job growth through 2018:** –5.2%.

Postal Service Clerks

Perform any combination of tasks in a post office, such as receiving letters and parcels; selling postage and revenue stamps, postal cards, and stamped envelopes; filling out and selling money orders; placing mail in pigeonholes of mail rack or in bags according to state, address, or other scheme; and examining mail for correct postage. **Skill levels:** *Low:* Artistic, communication, mathematics, mechanical. **Education and training:** Short-term on-the-job training. **Annual earnings:** $52,530. **Annual openings:** 1,610. **Job growth through 2018:** –18.0%.

Postal Service Mail Carriers

Sort mail for delivery and deliver mail on established route by vehicle or on foot. **Skill levels:** None met the criteria. **Education and training:** Short-term on-the-job training. **Annual earnings:** $52,200. **Annual openings:** 10,720. **Job growth through 2018:** –1.1%.

Postal Service Mail Sorters, Processors, and Processing Machine Operators

Prepare incoming and outgoing mail for distribution. **Skill levels:** *Low:* Mechanical. **Education and training:** Short-term on-the-job training. **Annual earnings:** $52,520. **Annual openings:** 1,660. **Job growth through 2018:** –30.3%.

Procurement Clerks

Compile information and records to draw up purchase orders for procurement of materials and services. **Skill levels:** *High:* Managerial. *Medium:* Communication, interpersonal, mathematics. *Low:* Science. **Education and training:** Moderate-term on-the-job training. **Annual earnings:** $36,110. **Annual openings:** 2,970. **Job growth through 2018:** 5.8%.

Receptionists and Information Clerks

Answer inquiries and obtain information for general public, customers, visitors, and other interested parties. **Skill levels:** *Medium:* Communication. *Low:* Interpersonal, managerial, mathematics, mechanical, science. **Education and training:** Short-term on-the-job training. **Annual earnings:** $25,070. **Annual openings:** 48,020. **Job growth through 2018:** 15.2%.

Secretaries and Administrative Assistants

Perform and coordinate an office's administrative activities and store, retrieve, and integrate information for dissemination to staff and clients. **Skill levels:** *Medium:* Communication. *Low:* Interpersonal, managerial, mathematics. **Education and training:** Moderate-term on-the-job training; work experience in a related occupation; associate degree. **Annual earnings:** $34,807. **Annual openings:** 105,750. **Job growth through 2018:** 10.8%.

Weighers, Measurers, Checkers, and Samplers, Recordkeeping

Weigh, measure, and check materials, supplies, and equipment for the purpose of keeping relevant records. **Skill levels:** *Medium:* Communication, mathematics, science. *Low:* Interpersonal. **Education and training:** Short-term on-the-job training. **Annual earnings:** $27,310. **Annual openings:** 2,510. **Job growth through 2018:** –13.1%.

Education/Training Usually Required: Postsecondary, Less Than Four Years

Secretaries and Administrative Assistants

Perform and coordinate an office's administrative activities and store, retrieve, and integrate information for dissemination to staff and clients. **Skill levels:** *Medium:* Communication. *Low:* Interpersonal, managerial, mathematics. **Education and training:** Moderate-term on-the-job training; work experience in a related occupation; associate degree. **Annual earnings:** $34,807. **Annual openings:** 105,750. **Job growth through 2018:** 10.8%.

Education/Training Usually Required: Bachelor's Degree or Higher

Accountants and Auditors

Examine, analyze, and interpret accounting records for the purpose of giving advice or preparing statements. **Skill levels:** *High:* Mathematics. *Medium:* Communication, interpersonal, managerial. **Education and training:** Bachelor's degree. **Annual earnings:** $60,340. **Annual openings:** 49,750. **Job growth through 2018:** 21.6%.

Administrative Services Managers

Plan, direct, or coordinate supportive services of an organization, such as recordkeeping, mail distribution, telephone operator/receptionist, and other office support services. **Skill levels:** *High:* Managerial. *Medium:* Communication, interpersonal, mathematics. *Low:* Mechanical, science. **Education and training:** Work experience plus degree. **Annual earnings:** $75,520. **Annual openings:** 8,660. **Job growth through 2018:** 12.5%.

Budget Analysts

Examine budget estimates for completeness, accuracy, and conformance with procedures and regulations. **Skill levels:** *Medium:* Managerial. *Low:* Artistic, communication, mathematics. **Education and training:** Bachelor's degree. **Annual earnings:** $66,660. **Annual openings:** 2,230. **Job growth through 2018:** 15.1%.

Human Resources, Training, and Labor Relations Managers and Specialists

Plan, direct, or coordinate activities and staff of an organization to deal with policies and practices for compensation, benefits, training, and development within the organization. **Skill levels:** *Medium:* Artistic, communication, interpersonal, managerial. *Low:* Mathematics. **Education and training:** Bachelor's degree; work experience plus degree. **Annual earnings:** $58,265. **Annual openings:** 42,730. **Job growth through 2018:** 21.8%.

Management Analysts

Conduct organizational studies and evaluations, design systems and procedures, conduct work simplifications and measurement studies, and prepare operations and procedures manuals to assist management in operating more efficiently and effectively. **Skill levels:** *High:* Communication, interpersonal, managerial, mechanical, science. *Medium:* Mathematics. *Low:* Artistic. **Education and training:** Work experience plus degree. **Annual earnings:** $75,250. **Annual openings:** 30,650. **Job growth through 2018:** 23.9%.

Top Executives

Devise strategies and formulate policies to ensure that organizations meet their goals and objectives. **Skill levels:** *High:* Managerial. *Medium:* Interpersonal. *Low:* Communication, mathematics. **Education and training:** Work experience plus degree. **Annual earnings:** $102,845. **Annual openings:** 61,470. **Job growth through 2018:** –0.4%.

5. Education and Training

Education/Training Usually Required: On-the-Job Training or Work Experience

Athletes, Coaches, Umpires, and Related Workers

Compete in, train for, recruit for, coach in, or officiate at professional athletic events. **Skill levels:** *High:* Interpersonal, managerial. *Medium:* Artistic, communication, mechanical, science. *Low:* Mathematics. **Education and training:** Long-term on-the-job training. **Annual earnings:** $28,761. **Annual openings:** 10,900. **Job growth through 2018:** 23.1%.

Interpreters and Translators

Translate or interpret written, oral, or sign language text into another language for others. **Skill levels:** *High:* Artistic. *Medium:* Communication. *Low:* Interpersonal, science. **Education and training:** Long-term on-the-job training. **Annual earnings:** $40,860. **Annual openings:** 2,340. **Job growth through 2018:** 22.2%.

Library Technicians and Library Assistants

Help librarians acquire, prepare, and organize materials and assist users in locating the appropriate resources. **Skill levels:** *Low:* Artistic, communication, mechanical. **Education and training:** Short-term on-the-job training; postsecondary vocational training. **Annual earnings:** $26,218. **Annual openings:** 12,890. **Job growth through 2018:** 10.0%.

Teacher Assistants

Perform duties that are instructional in nature or deliver direct services to students or parents. **Skill levels:** *Medium:* Artistic, communication, interpersonal, mathematics, science. **Education and training:** Short-term on-the-job training. **Annual earnings:** $22,820. **Annual openings:** 41,270. **Job growth through 2018:** 10.3%.

Teachers—Postsecondary

Instruct students in a wide variety of academic and vocational subjects beyond the high school level. **Skill levels:** *High:* Communication, interpersonal, managerial, mathematics, science. *Medium:* Artistic. *Low:* Mechanical. **Education and training:** Work experience in a related occupation; doctoral degree. **Annual earnings:** $63,263. **Annual openings:** 55,290. **Job growth through 2018:** 15.1%.

Teachers—Self-Enrichment Education

Provide instruction in a wide variety of subjects that students take for fun or self-improvement. **Skill levels:** *High:* Artistic. *Medium:* Communication, interpersonal. *Low:* Managerial, mechanical, science. **Education and training:** Work experience in a related occupation. **Annual earnings:** $36,440. **Annual openings:** 12,030. **Job growth through 2018:** 32.0%.

Education/Training Usually Required: Postsecondary, Less Than Four Years

Fitness Workers

Lead, instruct, and motivate individuals or groups in exercise activities, including cardiovascular exercise, strength training, and stretching. **Skill levels:** *High:* Science. *Medium:* Artistic, interpersonal, mechanical. *Low:* Communication, managerial. **Education and training:** Postsecondary vocational training. **Annual earnings:** $30,670. **Annual openings:** 12,380. **Job growth through 2018:** 29.4%.

Library Technicians and Library Assistants

Help librarians acquire, prepare, and organize materials and assist users in locating the appropriate resources. **Skill levels:** *Low:* Artistic, communication, mechanical. **Education and training:** Short-term on-the-job training; postsecondary vocational training. **Annual earnings:** $26,218. **Annual openings:** 12,890. **Job growth through 2018:** 10.0%.

Teachers—Preschool, Except Special Education

Nurture, teach, and care for children who have not yet entered kindergarten. **Skill levels:** *High:* Artistic. *Medium:* Interpersonal, science. *Low:* Communication, managerial, mechanical. **Education and training:** Postsecondary vocational training. **Annual earnings:** $24,540. **Annual openings:** 17,830. **Job growth through 2018:** 19.0%.

Education/Training Usually Required: Bachelor's Degree or Higher

Education Administrators

Provide instructional leadership and manage the day-to-day activities in schools, preschools, day care centers, and colleges and universities. **Skill levels:** *High:* Communication, interpersonal, managerial. *Medium:* Artistic, mathematics, science. *Low:* Mechanical. **Education and training:** Work experience plus degree. **Annual earnings:** $78,210. **Annual openings:** 17,040. **Job growth through 2018:** 8.3%.

Instructional Coordinators

Develop instructional material, coordinate educational content, and incorporate current technology in specialized fields that provide guidelines to educators and instructors for developing curricula and conducting courses. **Skill levels:** *High:* Artistic, communication, interpersonal, managerial. *Medium:* Mathematics, science. *Low:* Mechanical. **Education and training:** Master's degree. **Annual earnings:** $58,780. **Annual openings:** 6,060. **Job growth through 2018:** 23.2%.

Librarians

Administer libraries and perform related library services. **Skill levels:** *High:* Communication, interpersonal, managerial. *Medium:* Artistic, mathematics, mechanical, science. **Education and training:** Master's degree. **Annual earnings:** $53,710. **Annual openings:** 5,450. **Job growth through 2018:** 7.8%.

Teachers—Adult Literacy and Remedial Education

Instruct adults and out-of-school youths in reading, writing, speaking English, and math—skills to equip them to solve problems, improve their job opportunities, and further their education. **Skill levels:** *High:* Artistic, communication, interpersonal. *Medium:* Mathematics, science. *Low:* Managerial. **Education and training:** Bachelor's degree. **Annual earnings:** $45,920. **Annual openings:** 2,920. **Job growth through 2018:** 15.1%.

Teachers—Kindergarten, Elementary, Middle, and Secondary

Use classroom presentations or individual instruction to help students learn and apply concepts in subjects such as science, mathematics, and English. **Skill levels:** *High:* Artistic, communication, interpersonal. *Medium:* Managerial, mathematics, science. *Low:* Mechanical. **Education and training:** Bachelor's degree. **Annual earnings:** $50,949. **Annual openings:** 132,300. **Job growth through 2018:** 13.5%.

Teachers—Postsecondary

Instruct students in a wide variety of academic and vocational subjects beyond the high school level. **Skill levels:** *High:* Communication, interpersonal, managerial, mathematics, science. *Medium:* Artistic. *Low:* Mechanical. **Education and training:** Work experience in a related occupation; doctoral degree. **Annual earnings:** $63,263. **Annual openings:** 15.1%. **Job growth through 2018:** 55,290.

Teachers—Special Education

Instruct children and youths who have a variety of disabilities. **Skill levels:** *High:* Artistic, communication, interpersonal. *Medium:* Managerial, mathematics, science. **Education and training:** Bachelor's degree. **Annual earnings:** $51,766. **Annual openings:** 20,450. **Job growth through 2018:** 17.3%.

Teachers—Vocational

Instruct and train students to work in a wide variety of fields. **Skill levels:** *High:* Communication, interpersonal, managerial, mechanical, science. *Medium:* Artistic, mathematics. **Education and training:** Work experience plus degree. **Annual earnings:** $52,126. **Annual openings:** 4,260. **Job growth through 2018:** 8.8%.

6. Finance and Insurance

Education/Training Usually Required: On-the-Job Training or Work Experience

Bill and Account Collectors

Locate and notify customers of delinquent accounts by mail, telephone, or personal visit to solicit payment. **Skill levels:** *High:* Managerial. *Medium:* Communication, interpersonal, mathematics, mechanical. *Low:* Science. **Education and training:** Short-term on-the-job training. **Annual earnings:** $30,940. **Annual openings:** 15,690. **Job growth through 2018:** 19.3%.

Claims Adjusters, Appraisers, Examiners, and Investigators

Investigate insurance claims, negotiate settlements, and authorize payments to policyholders who make a claim. **Skill levels:** *High:* Communication, interpersonal. *Medium:* Managerial, mathematics. *Low:* Science. **Education and training:** Long-term on-the-job training; postsecondary vocational training. **Annual earnings:** $57,063. **Annual openings:** 9,860. **Job growth through 2018:** 6.8%.

Credit Authorizers, Checkers, and Clerks

Authorize credit charges against customers' accounts. **Skill levels:** *Medium:* Communication, mathematics. *Low:* Interpersonal, managerial. **Education and training:** Short-term on-the-job training. **Annual earnings:** $31,950. **Annual openings:** 1,990. **Job growth through 2018:** 2.8%.

Loan Interviewers and Clerks

Interview loan applicants to elicit information; investigate applicants' backgrounds and verify references; prepare loan request papers; and forward findings, reports, and documents to appraisal department. **Skill levels:** *Medium:* Communication, interpersonal, mathematics. *Low:* Managerial, mechanical, science. **Education and training:** Short-term on-the-job training. **Annual earnings:** $33,350. **Annual openings:** 6,090. **Job growth through 2018:** 4.3%.

Loan Officers

Evaluate, authorize, or recommend approval of commercial, real estate, or credit loans. **Skill levels:** *High:* Interpersonal. *Medium:* Communication. *Low:* Managerial, mathematics. **Education and training:** Moderate-term on-the-job training. **Annual earnings:** $54,880. **Annual openings:** 6,880. **Job growth through 2018:** 10.1%.

Tellers

Receive and pay out money; keep records of money and negotiable instruments involved in a financial institution's various transactions. **Skill levels:** *Medium:* Mathematics. *Low:* Mechanical. **Education and training:** Short-term on-the-job training. **Annual earnings:** $23,980. **Annual openings:** 28,440. **Job growth through 2018:** 6.2%.

Education/Training Usually Required: Postsecondary, Less Than Four Years

Claims Adjusters, Appraisers, Examiners, and Investigators

Investigate insurance claims, negotiate settlements, and authorize payments to policyholders who make a claim. **Skill levels:** *High:* Communication, interpersonal. *Medium:* Managerial, mathematics. *Low:* Science. **Education and training:** Long-term on-the-job training; postsecondary vocational training. **Annual earnings:** $57,063. **Annual openings:** 9,860. **Job growth through 2018:** 6.8%.

Insurance Sales Agents

Sell life, property, casualty, health, automotive, or other types of insurance. **Skill levels:** *High:* Communication, interpersonal, managerial, mathematics. *Low:* Artistic, mechanical. **Education and training:** Postsecondary vocational training. **Annual earnings:** $45,500. **Annual openings:** 15,260. **Job growth through 2018:** 11.9%.

Education/Training Usually Required: Bachelor's Degree or Higher

Actuaries

Analyze statistical data, such as mortality, accident, sickness, disability, and retirement rates, and construct probability tables to forecast risk and liability for payment of future benefits. **Skill levels:** *High:* Communication, interpersonal, mathematics, science. *Medium:* Managerial. *Low:* Artistic, mechanical. **Education and training:** Work experience plus degree. **Annual earnings:** $87,210. **Annual openings:** 1,000. **Job growth through 2018:** 21.4%.

Financial Analysts

Conduct quantitative analyses of information affecting investment programs of public or private institutions. **Skill levels:** *High:* Managerial, mathematics. *Medium:* Artistic, communication, interpersonal, science. *Low:* Mechanical. **Education and training:** Bachelor's degree. **Annual earnings:** $73,670. **Annual openings:** 9,520. **Job growth through 2018:** 19.8%.

Financial Managers

Plan, direct, and coordinate accounting, investing, banking, insurance, securities, and other financial activities of a branch, office, or department of an establishment. **Skill levels:** *High:* Communication, interpersonal, managerial, mathematics. *Low:* Mechanical, science. **Education and training:** Work experience plus degree. **Annual earnings:** $101,190. **Annual openings:** 13,820. **Job growth through 2018:** 7.6%.

Insurance Underwriters

Review individual applications for insurance to evaluate degree of risk involved and determine acceptance of applications. **Skill levels:** *High:* Communication. *Medium:* Interpersonal. *Low:* Managerial, mathematics, science. **Education and training:**

Bachelor's degree. **Annual earnings:** $57,820. **Annual openings:** 3,000. **Job growth through 2018:** –4.1%.

Personal Financial Advisors

Advise clients on financial plans, utilizing knowledge of tax and investment strategies, securities, insurance, pension plans, and real estate. **Skill levels:** *High:* Communication, managerial, mathematics. *Medium:* Interpersonal. *Low:* Artistic, science. **Education and training:** Bachelor's degree. **Annual earnings:** $68,200. **Annual openings:** 8,530. **Job growth through 2018:** 30.1%.

Securities, Commodities, and Financial Services Sales Agents

Buy and sell securities in investment and trading firms or call upon businesses and individuals to sell financial services. **Skill levels:** *High:* Communication, interpersonal, mathematics. *Medium:* Managerial. *Low:* Artistic, science. **Education and training:** Bachelor's degree. **Annual earnings:** $66,930. **Annual openings:** 12,680. **Job growth through 2018:** 9.3%.

7. Government and Public Administration

Education/Training Usually Required: On-the-Job Training or Work Experience

No occupations at this level.

Education/Training Usually Required: Postsecondary, Less Than Four Years

No occupations at this level.

Education/Training Usually Required: Bachelor's Degree or Higher

Tax Examiners, Collectors, and Revenue Agents

Determine tax liability or collect taxes from individuals or business firms according to prescribed laws and regulations. **Skill levels:** *High:* Mathematics. *Medium:* Communication. *Low:* Managerial. **Education and training:** Bachelor's degree. **Annual earnings:** $48,550. **Annual openings:** 3,520. **Job growth through 2018:** 13.0%.

Urban and Regional Planners

Develop long- and short-term plans for the use of land and the growth and revitalization of urban, suburban, and rural communities and the region in which they are located. **Skill levels:** *High:* Artistic, communication, interpersonal. *Medium:* Managerial, mathematics, science. **Education and training:** Master's degree. **Annual earnings:** $61,820. **Annual openings:** 1,470. **Job growth through 2018:** 19.0%.

8. Health Science

Education/Training Usually Required: On-the-Job Training or Work Experience

Dental Assistants

Help dentist, setting up patients and equipment and keeping records. **Skill levels:** *High:* Mechanical. *Medium:* Communication, interpersonal, managerial, science. *Low:* Artistic. **Education and training:** Moderate-term on-the-job training. **Annual earnings:** $33,230. **Annual openings:** 16,100. **Job growth through 2018:** 35.7%.

Medical Assistants

Perform administrative and clinical tasks to keep the offices of physicians, podiatrists, chiropractors, and other health practitioners running smoothly. **Skill levels:** *Low:* Artistic, communication, interpersonal. **Education and training:** Moderate-term on-the-job training. **Annual earnings:** $28,650. **Annual openings:** 21,780. **Job growth through 2018:** 33.9%.

Medical, Dental, and Ophthalmic Laboratory Technicians

Following the specifications of health-care professionals, produce a variety of implements to help patients with daily tasks such as seeing well, walking, and chewing food. **Skill levels:** *High:* Mechanical. *Medium:* Artistic, managerial, science. *Low:* Communication, interpersonal, mathematics. **Education and training:** Moderate-term on-the-job training; long-term on-the-job training. **Annual earnings:** $32,471. **Annual openings:** 3,150. **Job growth through 2018:** 13.8%.

Nursing and Psychiatric Aides

Help care for physically or mentally ill, injured, disabled, or infirm individuals in hospitals, nursing care facilities, and mental health settings. **Skill levels:** *Low:* Artistic. **Education and training:** Short-term on-the-job training; postsecondary vocational training. **Annual earnings:** $24,107. **Annual openings:** 43,210. **Job growth through 2018:** 18.2%.

Occupational Therapist Assistants and Aides

Work under the direction of occupational therapists to provide rehabilitative services to persons with mental, physical, emotional, or developmental impairments. **Skill levels:** *High:* Interpersonal. *Medium:* Artistic, communication, mechanical, science. *Low:* Managerial, mathematics. **Education and training:** Short-term on-the-job training; associate degree. **Annual earnings:** $44,572. **Annual openings:** 1,530. **Job growth through 2018:** 30.0%.

Opticians, Dispensing

Design, measure, fit, and adapt lenses and frames for client according to written optical prescription or specification. **Skill levels:** *High:* Science. *Medium:* Communication, interpersonal, managerial, mathematics, mechanical. *Low:* Artistic. **Education and training:** Long-term on-the-job training. **Annual earnings:** $32,740. **Annual openings:** 2,020. **Job growth through 2018:** 13.4%.

Pharmacy Technicians and Aides

Help licensed pharmacists prepare prescription medications, provide customer service, and perform administrative duties within a pharmacy setting. **Skill levels:** *Medium:* Communication, mathematics, science. *Low:* Mechanical. **Education and training:** Short-term on-the-job training; moderate-term on-the-job training. **Annual earnings:** $27,081. **Annual openings:** 18,810. **Job growth through 2018:** 25.3%.

Physical Therapist Assistants and Aides

Help physical therapists to provide treatment that improves patient mobility, relieves pain, and prevents or lessens physical disabilities of patients. **Skill levels:** *Low:* Artistic, interpersonal. **Education and training:** Short-term on-the-job training; associate degree. **Annual earnings:** $38,305. **Annual openings:** 5,390. **Job growth through 2018:** 34.5%.

Social and Human Service Assistants

Assist professionals from a wide variety of fields, such as psychology, rehabilitation, or social work, to provide client services, as well as support for families. **Skill levels:** *Medium:* Interpersonal. *Low:* Artistic, communication, managerial. **Education and training:** Moderate-term on-the-job training. **Annual earnings:** $27,940. **Annual openings:** 15,390. **Job growth through 2018:** 22.6%.

Education/Training Usually Required: Postsecondary, Less Than Four Years

Cardiovascular Technologists and Technicians

Assist physicians in diagnosing and treating cardiac (heart) and peripheral vascular (blood vessel) ailments. **Skill levels:** *Low:* Artistic, communication, mechanical, science. **Education and training:** Associate degree. **Annual earnings:** $48,300. **Annual openings:** 1,910. **Job growth through 2018:** 24.1%.

Clinical Laboratory Technologists and Technicians

Perform laboratory tests that aid in the detection, diagnosis, and treatment of disease. **Skill levels:** *High:* Mechanical, science. *Medium:* Artistic, communication, mathematics. *Low:* Interpersonal, managerial. **Education and training:** Associate degree; bachelor's degree. **Annual earnings:** $46,017. **Annual openings:** 10,790. **Job growth through 2018:** 13.9%.

Dental Hygienists

Clean teeth and examine oral areas, head, and neck for signs of oral disease. **Skill levels:** *High:* Communication, science. *Medium:* Interpersonal, mechanical. **Education and training:** Associate degree. **Annual earnings:** $67,340. **Annual openings:** 9,840. **Job growth through 2018:** 36.1%.

Diagnostic Medical Sonographers

Produce ultrasonic recordings of internal organs for use by physicians. **Skill levels:** *Medium:* Mechanical. *Low:* Artistic, communication, interpersonal, science.

Education and training: Associate degree. **Annual earnings:** $63,010. **Annual openings:** 1,650. **Job growth through 2018:** 18.3%.

Emergency Medical Technicians and Paramedics

Assess injuries, administer emergency medical care, and extricate trapped individuals. **Skill levels:** *Low:* Artistic, interpersonal, managerial. **Education and training:** Postsecondary vocational training. **Annual earnings:** $30,000. **Annual openings:** 6,200. **Job growth through 2018:** 9.0%.

Licensed Practical and Licensed Vocational Nurses

Care for people who are sick, injured, convalescent, or disabled. **Skill levels:** *Low:* Artistic, interpersonal, science. **Education and training:** Postsecondary vocational training. **Annual earnings:** $39,820. **Annual openings:** 39,130. **Job growth through 2018:** 20.6%.

Massage Therapists

Massage customers for hygienic or remedial purposes. **Skill levels:** *Low:* Artistic, communication, science. **Education and training:** Postsecondary vocational training. **Annual earnings:** $35,230. **Annual openings:** 3,950. **Job growth through 2018:** 18.9%.

Medical Records and Health Information Technicians

Compile, process, and maintain medical records of hospital and clinic patients in a manner consistent with medical, administrative, ethical, legal, and regulatory requirements of the health-care system. **Skill levels:** None met the criteria. **Education and training:** Associate degree. **Annual earnings:** $31,290. **Annual openings:** 7,030. **Job growth through 2018:** 20.3%.

Medical Transcriptionists

Use transcribing machines with headset and foot pedal to listen to recordings by physicians and other health-care professionals dictating a variety of medical reports, such as emergency room visits, diagnostic imaging studies, operations, chart reviews, and final summaries. **Skill levels:** *Medium:* Artistic, communication. *Low:* Mechanical. **Education and training:** Postsecondary vocational training. **Annual earnings:** $32,600. **Annual openings:** 2,350. **Job growth through 2018:** 11.2%.

Nuclear Medicine Technologists

Prepare, administer, and measure radioactive isotopes in therapeutic, diagnostic, and tracer studies, utilizing a variety of radioisotope equipment. **Skill levels:** *Medium:* Science. *Low:* Artistic, mechanical. **Education and training:** Associate degree. **Annual earnings:** $67,910. **Annual openings:** 670. **Job growth through 2018:** 16.3%.

Nursing and Psychiatric Aides

Help care for physically or mentally ill, injured, disabled, or infirm individuals in hospitals, nursing care facilities, and mental health settings. **Skill levels:** *Low:*

Artistic. **Education and training:** Short-term on-the-job training; postsecondary vocational training. **Annual earnings:** $24,107. **Annual openings:** 43,210. **Job growth through 2018:** 18.2%.

Occupational Therapist Assistants and Aides

Work under the direction of occupational therapists to provide rehabilitative services to persons with mental, physical, emotional, or developmental impairments. **Skill levels:** *High:* Interpersonal. *Medium:* Artistic, communication, mechanical, science. *Low:* Managerial, mathematics. **Education and training:** Short-term on-the-job training; associate degree. **Annual earnings:** $44,572. **Annual openings:** 1,530. **Job growth through 2018:** 30.0%.

Physical Therapist Assistants and Aides

Help physical therapists to provide treatment that improves patient mobility, relieves pain, and prevents or lessens physical disabilities of patients. **Skill levels:** *Low:* Artistic, interpersonal. **Education and training:** Short-term on-the-job training; associate degree. **Annual earnings:** $38,305. **Annual openings:** 5,390. **Job growth through 2018:** 34.5%.

Radiation Therapists

Provide radiation therapy to patients as prescribed by a radiologist according to established practices and standards. **Skill levels:** *Medium:* Mechanical. *Low:* Communication, mathematics, science. **Education and training:** Associate degree. **Annual earnings:** $74,170. **Annual openings:** 690. **Job growth through 2018:** 27.1%.

Radiologic Technologists and Technicians

Take X-rays and CAT scans or administer nonradioactive materials into patients' bloodstreams for diagnostic purposes. **Skill levels:** *Medium:* Communication, science. *Low:* Artistic, interpersonal, mathematics, mechanical. **Education and training:** Associate degree. **Annual earnings:** $53,240. **Annual openings:** 6,800. **Job growth through 2018:** 17.2%.

Registered Nurses

Administer nursing care to ill, injured, convalescent, or disabled patients. **Skill levels:** *Medium:* Artistic, interpersonal, managerial, science. *Low:* Communication, mathematics. **Education and training:** Associate degree. **Annual earnings:** $63,750. **Annual openings:** 103,900. **Job growth through 2018:** 22.2%.

Respiratory Therapists

Evaluate, treat, and care for patients with breathing or other cardiopulmonary disorders. **Skill levels:** *High:* Mathematics, science. *Medium:* Communication, mechanical. *Low:* Artistic, interpersonal, managerial. **Education and training:** Associate degree. **Annual earnings:** $53,330. **Annual openings:** 4,140. **Job growth through 2018:** 20.9%.

Respiratory Therapy Technicians

Provide specific, well-defined respiratory care procedures under the direction of respiratory therapists and physicians. **Skill levels:** *High:* Communication, interpersonal, managerial, mathematics, mechanical, science. *Low:* Artistic. **Education and training:** Postsecondary vocational training. **Annual earnings:** $44,700. **Annual openings:** 420. **Job growth through 2018:** –1.1%.

Surgical Technologists

Assist in operations under the supervision of surgeons, registered nurses, or other surgical personnel. **Skill levels:** *Medium:* Mechanical. *Low:* Interpersonal, managerial, science. **Education and training:** Postsecondary vocational training. **Annual earnings:** $39,400. **Annual openings:** 4,630. **Job growth through 2018:** 25.3%.

Veterinary Technologists and Technicians

Perform medical tests in a laboratory environment for use in the treatment and diagnosis of diseases in animals. **Skill levels:** *High:* Mathematics, science. *Medium:* Communication, interpersonal, managerial, mechanical. *Low:* Artistic. **Education and training:** Associate degree. **Annual earnings:** $29,280. **Annual openings:** 4,850. **Job growth through 2018:** 35.8%.

Education/Training Usually Required: Bachelor's Degree or Higher

Athletic Trainers

Evaluate, advise, and treat athletes to assist recovery from injury, avoid injury, or maintain peak physical fitness. **Skill levels:** *High:* Communication, interpersonal, managerial, mechanical, science. *Medium:* Artistic, mathematics. **Education and training:** Bachelor's degree. **Annual earnings:** $41,340. **Annual openings:** 1,150. **Job growth through 2018:** 36.9%.

Audiologists

Assess and treat persons with hearing and related disorders. **Skill levels:** *High:* Communication, interpersonal, managerial, mechanical, science. *Medium:* Artistic, mathematics. **Education and training:** First professional degree. **Annual earnings:** $63,230. **Annual openings:** 580. **Job growth through 2018:** 25.0%.

Chiropractors

Adjust spinal column and other articulations of the body to correct abnormalities of the human body believed to be caused by interference with the nervous system. **Skill levels:** *Medium:* Artistic. *Low:* Communication, interpersonal, managerial, science. **Education and training:** First professional degree. **Annual earnings:** $67,650. **Annual openings:** 1,820. **Job growth through 2018:** 19.5%.

Clinical Laboratory Technologists and Technicians

Perform laboratory tests that aid in the detection, diagnosis, and treatment of disease. **Skill levels:** *High:* Mechanical, science. *Medium:* Artistic, communication, mathematics. *Low:* Interpersonal, managerial. **Education and training:** Associate degree;

bachelor's degree. **Annual earnings:** $46,017. **Annual openings:** 10,790. **Job growth through 2018:** 13.9%.

Dentists

Diagnose and treat problems with teeth and tissues in the mouth, giving advice and administering care to help prevent future problems. **Skill levels:** *High:* Communication, interpersonal, managerial, mechanical, science. *Medium:* Artistic, mathematics. **Education and training:** First professional degree. **Annual earnings:** $142,478. **Annual openings:** 6,150. **Job growth through 2018:** 15.6%.

Dietitians and Nutritionists

Plan and conduct food service or nutritional programs to assist in the promotion of health and control of disease. **Skill levels:** *High:* Communication, science. *Medium:* Artistic, interpersonal, mathematics. *Low:* Managerial, mechanical. **Education and training:** Bachelor's degree. **Annual earnings:** $52,150. **Annual openings:** 2,570. **Job growth through 2018:** 9.2%.

Medical and Health Services Managers

Plan, direct, or coordinate medicine and health services in hospitals, clinics, managed care organizations, public health agencies, or similar organizations. **Skill levels:** *High:* Managerial. *Medium:* Interpersonal. *Low:* Artistic, communication, mathematics. **Education and training:** Work experience plus degree. **Annual earnings:** $81,850. **Annual openings:** 9,940. **Job growth through 2018:** 16.0%.

Occupational Health and Safety Specialists

Review, evaluate, and analyze work environments and design programs and procedures to control, eliminate, and prevent disease or injury caused by chemical, physical, and biological agents or ergonomic factors. **Skill levels:** *High:* Communication, interpersonal, managerial, mathematics, science. *Medium:* Mechanical. *Low:* Artistic. **Education and training:** Bachelor's degree. **Annual earnings:** $63,230. **Annual openings:** 2,490. **Job growth through 2018:** 11.2%.

Occupational Therapists

Help patients improve their ability to perform tasks in living and working environments. **Skill levels:** *Medium:* Artistic. *Low:* Communication, interpersonal, managerial, science. **Education and training:** Master's degree. **Annual earnings:** $69,630. **Annual openings:** 4,580. **Job growth through 2018:** 25.6%.

Optometrists

Diagnose, manage, and treat conditions and diseases of the human eye and visual system. **Skill levels:** *Medium:* Managerial. *Low:* Communication, interpersonal, mathematics, science. **Education and training:** First professional degree. **Annual earnings:** $96,140. **Annual openings:** 2,010. **Job growth through 2018:** 24.4%.

Pharmacists

Compound and dispense medications following prescriptions issued by physicians, dentists, or other authorized medical practitioners. **Skill levels:** *High:*

Communication, mathematics, science. *Medium:* Interpersonal. *Low:* Artistic, managerial, mechanical. **Education and training:** First professional degree. **Annual earnings:** $109,180. **Annual openings:** 10,580. **Job growth through 2018:** 17.0%.

Physical Therapists

Assess, plan, organize, and participate in rehabilitative programs that improve mobility, relieve pain, increase strength, and decrease or prevent deformity of patients suffering from disease or injury. **Skill levels:** *Medium:* Artistic. *Low:* Communication, interpersonal, managerial, science. **Education and training:** Master's degree. **Annual earnings:** $74,480. **Annual openings:** 7,860. **Job growth through 2018:** 30.3%.

Physician Assistants

Practice medicine under the supervision of physicians and surgeons. **Skill levels:** *Medium:* Communication, interpersonal. *Low:* Artistic, mathematics, science. **Education and training:** Master's degree. **Annual earnings:** $84,420. **Annual openings:** 4,280. **Job growth through 2018:** 39.0%.

Physicians and Surgeons

Diagnose illnesses and prescribe and administer treatment for people suffering from injury or disease. **Skill levels:** *High:* Communication, interpersonal, managerial, science. *Medium:* Artistic, mathematics, mechanical. **Education and training:** First professional degree. **Annual earnings:** $158,865. **Annual openings:** 21.8%. **Job growth through 2018:** 26,050.

Podiatrists

Diagnose and treat diseases and deformities of the human foot. **Skill levels:** *High:* Communication, interpersonal, managerial, mathematics, science. *Medium:* Artistic, mechanical. **Education and training:** First professional degree. **Annual earnings:** $116,250. **Annual openings:** 320. **Job growth through 2018:** 9.0%.

Recreational Therapists

Plan, direct, or coordinate medically approved recreation programs for patients in hospitals, nursing homes, or other institutions. **Skill levels:** *High:* Artistic. *Medium:* Interpersonal. *Low:* Communication, managerial. **Education and training:** Bachelor's degree. **Annual earnings:** $39,440. **Annual openings:** 1,160. **Job growth through 2018:** 14.6%.

Speech-Language Pathologists

Assess and treat persons with speech, language, voice, and fluency disorders. **Skill levels:** *High:* Artistic, communication, interpersonal, science. *Medium:* Managerial, mathematics. *Low:* Mechanical. **Education and training:** Master's degree. **Annual earnings:** $65,090. **Annual openings:** 4,380. **Job growth through 2018:** 18.5%.

Veterinarians

Diagnose and treat diseases and dysfunctions of animals. **Skill levels:** *High:* Communication, interpersonal, managerial, mathematics, mechanical, science. *Medium:* Artistic. **Education and training:** First professional degree. **Annual earnings:** $80,510. **Annual openings:** 3,020. **Job growth through 2018:** 32.9%.

9. Hospitality, Tourism, and Recreation

Education/Training Usually Required: On-the-Job Training or Work Experience

Building Cleaning Workers

Keep office buildings, hospitals, stores, apartment houses, hotels, and residences clean, sanitary, and in good condition. **Skill levels:** *Medium:* Mechanical. *Low:* Science. **Education and training:** Short-term on-the-job training; work experience in a related occupation. **Annual earnings:** $21,949. **Annual openings:** 95,080. **Job growth through 2018:** 4.9%.

Chefs, Head Cooks, and Food Preparation and Serving Supervisors

Oversee the daily food service operation of a restaurant or other food service establishment. **Skill levels:** *Medium:* Artistic, managerial, mechanical, science. *Low:* Communication, interpersonal, mathematics. **Education and training:** Work experience in a related occupation. **Annual earnings:** $30,600. **Annual openings:** 14,520. **Job growth through 2018:** 5.9%.

Cooks and Food Preparation Workers

Prepare, season, and cook a wide range of foods—from soups, snacks, and salads to entrees, side dishes, and desserts. **Skill levels:** *Medium:* Mechanical. *Low:* Artistic, managerial, science. **Education and training:** Short-term on-the-job training; moderate-term on-the-job training; long-term on-the-job training. **Annual earnings:** $20,305. **Annual openings:** 73,520. **Job growth through 2018:** 5.9%.

Food and Beverage Serving and Related Workers

Serve customers in full-service restaurants, casual dining eateries, and other food service establishments. **Skill levels:** *Medium:* Artistic. *Low:* Mechanical. **Education and training:** Short-term on-the-job training. **Annual earnings:** $17,685. **Annual openings:** 391,590. **Job growth through 2018:** 9.9%.

Food Service Managers

Plan, direct, or coordinate activities of an organization or department that serves food and beverages. **Skill levels:** *High:* Managerial. *Medium:* Interpersonal. *Low:* Artistic, mechanical. **Education and training:** Work experience in a related occupation. **Annual earnings:** $47,210. **Annual openings:** 8,370. **Job growth through 2018:** 5.3%.

Lodging Managers

Plan, direct, or coordinate activities of an organization or department that provides lodging and other accommodations. **Skill levels:** *High:* Communication, interpersonal, managerial. *Low:* Artistic, mathematics, mechanical, science. **Education and training:** Work experience in a related occupation. **Annual earnings:** $46,300. **Annual openings:** 1,560. **Job growth through 2018:** 4.7%.

Reservation and Transportation Ticket Agents and Travel Clerks

Make and confirm reservations and sell tickets to passengers and for large hotel or motel chains. **Skill levels:** *Low:* Artistic, communication, interpersonal, managerial, mathematics, mechanical, science. **Education and training:** Short-term on-the-job training. **Annual earnings:** $31,250. **Annual openings:** 5,150. **Job growth through 2018:** 8.1%.

Education/Training Usually Required: Postsecondary, Less Than Four Years

Travel Agents

Plan and sell transportation and accommodations for travel agency customers. **Skill levels:** *Medium:* Artistic, communication, interpersonal, managerial, mathematics. *Low:* Mechanical. **Education and training:** Postsecondary vocational training. **Annual earnings:** $30,790. **Annual openings:** 790. **Job growth through 2018:** −1.1%.

Education/Training Usually Required: Bachelor's Degree or Higher

No occupations at this level.

10. Human Service

Education/Training Usually Required: On-the-Job Training or Work Experience

Barbers, Cosmetologists, and Other Personal Appearance Workers

Provide a wide range of services that help clients look and feel their best. **Skill levels:** *High:* Artistic, science. *Medium:* Managerial. *Low:* Interpersonal, mechanical. **Education and training:** Short-term on-the-job training; postsecondary vocational training. **Annual earnings:** $23,061. **Annual openings:** 28,580. **Job growth through 2018:** 20.1%.

Child Care Workers

Attend to children at schools, businesses, private households, and child care institutions. **Skill levels:** *High:* Artistic. *Medium:* Interpersonal. *Low:* Communication, managerial, mechanical, science. **Education and training:** Short-term on-the-job training. **Annual earnings:** $19,240. **Annual openings:** 52,310. **Job growth through 2018:** 10.9%.

Eligibility Interviewers, Government Programs

Determine eligibility of persons applying to receive assistance from government programs and agency resources, such as welfare, unemployment benefits, social security, and public housing. **Skill levels:** *Medium:* Communication. *Low:* Artistic, interpersonal, managerial, mathematics, mechanical. **Education and training:** Moderate-term on-the-job training. **Annual earnings:** $40,180. **Annual openings:** 3,880. **Job growth through 2018:** 9.2%.

Home Health Aides and Personal and Home Care Aides

Assist elderly or disabled adults with daily living activities at the person's home or in a daytime nonresidential facility. **Skill levels:** *Medium:* Artistic, interpersonal. *Low:* Communication, mechanical, science. **Education and training:** Short-term on-the-job training. **Annual earnings:** $20,162. **Annual openings:** 103,050. **Job growth through 2018:** 48.1%.

Recreation Workers

Conduct recreation activities with groups in public, private, or volunteer agencies or recreation facilities. **Skill levels:** *High:* Artistic, communication, interpersonal, managerial. *Medium:* Science. *Low:* Mathematics, mechanical. **Education and training:** Short-term on-the-job training. **Annual earnings:** $22,280. **Annual openings:** 10,720. **Job growth through 2018:** 14.7%.

Education/Training Usually Required: Postsecondary, Less Than Four Years

Barbers, Cosmetologists, and Other Personal Appearance Workers

Provide a wide range of services that help clients look and feel their best. **Skill levels:** *High:* Artistic, science. *Medium:* Managerial. *Low:* Interpersonal, mechanical. **Education and training:** Short-term on-the-job training; postsecondary vocational training. **Annual earnings:** $23,061. **Annual openings:** 28,580. **Job growth through 2018:** 20.1%.

Funeral Directors

Perform various tasks to arrange and direct funeral services, such as coordinating transportation of body to mortuary for embalming, interviewing family or other authorized person to arrange details, selecting pallbearers, procuring official for religious rites, and providing transportation for mourners. **Skill levels:** *Medium:* Interpersonal, managerial. *Low:* Artistic, communication, mathematics. **Education and training:** Associate degree. **Annual earnings:** $54,370. **Annual openings:** 960. **Job growth through 2018:** 11.9%.

Theatrical and Performance Makeup Artists

Apply makeup to enhance performing artists' appearances for movie, television, or stage performances. **Skill levels:** *High:* Artistic, managerial. *Medium:*

Communication, interpersonal, mechanical, science. **Education and training:** Postsecondary vocational training. **Annual earnings:** $31,450. **Annual openings:** 90. **Job growth through 2018:** 17.0%.

Education/Training Usually Required: Bachelor's Degree or Higher

Counselors

Work in diverse community settings designed to provide various counseling, rehabilitation, and support services. **Skill levels:** *High:* Communication, interpersonal. *Medium:* Artistic, managerial, science. **Education and training:** Bachelor's degree; master's degree. **Annual earnings:** $43,282. **Annual openings:** 25,130. **Job growth through 2018:** 17.5%.

Health Educators

Promote, maintain, and improve individual and community health by assisting individuals and communities in adopting healthy behaviors. **Skill levels:** *High:* Communication, interpersonal. *Medium:* Artistic, managerial. *Low:* Mechanical, science. **Education and training:** Bachelor's degree. **Annual earnings:** $44,340. **Annual openings:** 2,600. **Job growth through 2018:** 18.2%.

Probation Officers and Correctional Treatment Specialists

Provide social services to assist in rehabilitation of law offenders in custody or on probation or parole. **Skill levels:** *High:* Communication, interpersonal. *Medium:* Artistic, managerial, mathematics, science. *Low:* Mechanical. **Education and training:** Bachelor's degree. **Annual earnings:** $46,530. **Annual openings:** 4,180. **Job growth through 2018:** 19.3%.

Psychologists

Study mental processes and human behavior by observing, interpreting, and recording how people and other animals relate to one another and the environment. **Skill levels:** *High:* Artistic, communication, interpersonal, science. *Medium:* Managerial, mathematics. **Education and training:** Master's degree; doctoral degree. **Annual earnings:** $68,214. **Annual openings:** 6,800. **Job growth through 2018:** 11.6%.

Social Workers

Assist people by helping them cope with and solve issues in their everyday lives, such as family and personal problems and dealing with relationships. **Skill levels:** *High:* Communication, interpersonal. *Medium:* Artistic. *Low:* Managerial, science. **Education and training:** Bachelor's degree; master's degree. **Annual earnings:** $42,111. **Annual openings:** 26,460. **Job growth through 2018:** 16.1%.

11. Information Technology

Education/Training Usually Required: On-the-Job Training or Work Experience

Computer Operators

Monitor and control electronic computer and peripheral electronic data processing equipment to process business, scientific, engineering, and other data according to operating instructions. **Skill levels:** *Medium:* Mathematics, mechanical. *Low:* Communication, interpersonal, managerial, science. **Education and training:** Moderate-term on-the-job training. **Annual earnings:** $36,110. **Annual openings:** 1,240. **Job growth through 2018:** −18.6%.

Education/Training Usually Required: Postsecondary, Less Than Four Years

Computer Network, Systems, and Database Administrators

Help individuals and organizations share and store information through computer networks and systems, the Internet, and computer databases. **Skill levels:** *High:* Managerial, mechanical. *Medium:* Artistic, communication, interpersonal, mathematics, science. **Education and training:** Associate degree; bachelor's degree. **Annual earnings:** $71,726. **Annual openings:** 46,080. **Job growth through 2018:** 29.8%.

Computer Support Specialists

Provide technical assistance to computer system users. **Skill levels:** *Medium:* Mechanical. *Low:* Artistic, communication, interpersonal. **Education and training:** Associate degree. **Annual earnings:** $44,300. **Annual openings:** 23,460. **Job growth through 2018:** 13.8%.

Education/Training Usually Required: Bachelor's Degree or Higher

Computer and Information Systems Managers

Plan, direct, or coordinate activities in such fields as electronic data processing, information systems, systems analysis, and computer programming. **Skill levels:** *High:* Managerial. *Medium:* Mechanical. *Low:* Artistic, communication, interpersonal. **Education and training:** Work experience plus degree. **Annual earnings:** $113,720. **Annual openings:** 9,710. **Job growth through 2018:** 16.9%.

Computer Network, Systems, and Database Administrators

Help individuals and organizations share and store information through computer networks and systems, the Internet, and computer databases. **Skill levels:** *High:* Managerial, mechanical. *Medium:* Artistic, communication, interpersonal, mathematics, science. **Education and training:** Associate degree; bachelor's degree. **Annual earnings:** $71,726. **Annual openings:** 46,080. **Job growth through 2018:** 29.8%.

Computer Scientists

Conduct research and develop theoretical concepts to improve computer systems and the way they store and retrieve information. **Skill levels:** *High:* Artistic, communication, interpersonal, managerial, mathematics, science. *Medium:* Mechanical. **Education and training:** Doctoral degree. **Annual earnings:** $101,570. **Annual openings:** 1,320. **Job growth through 2018:** 24.2%.

Computer Software Engineers and Computer Programmers

Apply the theories and principles of computer science and mathematical analysis to create, test, and evaluate the software applications and systems that make computers work. **Skill levels:** *High:* Communication, mathematics, mechanical, science. *Medium:* Artistic, interpersonal. *Low:* Managerial. **Education and training:** Bachelor's degree. **Annual earnings:** $84,455. **Annual openings:** 45,210. **Job growth through 2018:** 21.2%.

Computer Systems Analysts

Analyze data processing problems in science, engineering, and business and devise ways to automate or improve existing systems. **Skill levels:** *High:* Mathematics, mechanical. *Medium:* Artistic, communication, interpersonal, managerial, science. **Education and training:** Bachelor's degree. **Annual earnings:** $77,080. **Annual openings:** 22,280. **Job growth through 2018:** 20.3%.

12. Law and Public Safety

Education/Training Usually Required: On-the-Job Training or Work Experience

Correctional Officers

Oversee individuals who have been arrested and are awaiting trial or who have been convicted of a crime and sentenced to serve time in a jail, reformatory, or penitentiary. **Skill levels:** *Medium:* Interpersonal. **Education and training:** Moderate-term on-the-job training; work experience in a related occupation. **Annual earnings:** $40,652. **Annual openings:** 16,920. **Job growth through 2018:** 9.3%.

Fire Fighters

Control and extinguish fires or respond to emergency situations where life, property, or the environment is at risk. **Skill levels:** *High:* Interpersonal, managerial, mechanical, science. *Medium:* Communication, mathematics. **Education and training:** Long-term on-the-job training; work experience in a related occupation. **Annual earnings:** $48,738. **Annual openings:** 18,530. **Job growth through 2018:** 17.0%.

Fire Inspectors and Investigators

Inspect buildings to detect fire hazards and enforce local ordinances and state laws. **Skill levels:** *High:* Communication, interpersonal, managerial, mathematics, mechanical, science. **Education and training:** Work experience in a related occupation. **Annual earnings:** $51,388. **Annual openings:** 610. **Job growth through 2018:** 9.2%.

Police and Detectives

Pursue and apprehend individuals who break the law and then issue citations or give warnings. **Skill levels:** *High:* Interpersonal. *Medium:* Communication. *Low:* Managerial, mathematics, mechanical, science. **Education and training:** Long-term on-the-job training; work experience in a related occupation; associate degree. **Annual earnings:** $56,994. **Annual openings:** 32,390. **Job growth through 2018:** 9.6%.

Police, Fire, and Ambulance Dispatchers

Receive complaints from the public concerning crimes and police emergencies. **Skill levels:** *Low:* Interpersonal. **Education and training:** Moderate-term on-the-job training. **Annual earnings:** $34,790. **Annual openings:** 3,840. **Job growth through 2018:** 17.8%.

Private Detectives and Investigators

Detect occurrences of unlawful acts or infractions of rules in private establishment or seek, examine, and compile information for client. **Skill levels:** *High:* Communication, interpersonal, managerial. *Medium:* Science. *Low:* Artistic, mathematics, mechanical. **Education and training:** Work experience in a related occupation. **Annual earnings:** $42,110. **Annual openings:** 1,930. **Job growth through 2018:** 22.0%.

Security Guards and Gaming Surveillance Officers

Patrol and inspect property to protect against fire, theft, vandalism, terrorism, and illegal activity. **Skill levels:** *Low:* Artistic. **Education and training:** Short-term on-the-job training; moderate-term on-the-job training. **Annual earnings:** $23,867. **Annual openings:** 37,690. **Job growth through 2018:** 14.1%.

Education/Training Usually Required: Postsecondary, Less Than Four Years

Court Reporters

Use verbatim methods and equipment to capture, store, retrieve, and transcribe pre-trial and trial proceedings or other information. **Skill levels:** *Medium:* Artistic, communication, mechanical. *Low:* Managerial, mathematics. **Education and training:** Postsecondary vocational training. **Annual earnings:** $47,810. **Annual openings:** 710. **Job growth through 2018:** 18.3%.

Paralegals and Legal Assistants

Assist lawyers by researching legal precedent, investigating facts, or preparing legal documents. **Skill levels:** *Medium:* Communication. *Low:* Artistic, managerial, mathematics. **Education and training:** Associate degree. **Annual earnings:** $46,980. **Annual openings:** 10,400. **Job growth through 2018:** 28.1%.

Police and Detectives

Pursue and apprehend individuals who break the law and then issue citations or give warnings. **Skill levels:** *High:* Interpersonal. *Medium:* Communication. *Low:* Managerial, mathematics, mechanical, science. **Education and training:** Long-term on-the-job training; work experience in a related occupation; associate degree. **Annual earnings:** $56,994. **Annual openings:** 32,390. **Job growth through 2018:** 9.6%.

Education/Training Usually Required: Bachelor's Degree or Higher

Judges, Magistrates, and Other Judicial Workers

Apply the law and oversee the legal process in courts. **Skill levels:** *High:* Communication, interpersonal. *Medium:* Artistic, managerial, mathematics, science. **Education and training:** Work experience plus degree. **Annual earnings:** $94,616. **Annual openings:** 1,200. **Job growth through 2018:** 3.6%.

Lawyers

Represent clients in criminal and civil litigation and other legal proceedings, draw up legal documents, and manage or advise clients on legal transactions. **Skill levels:** *High:* Artistic, communication, interpersonal, managerial. *Medium:* Mathematics, science. **Education and training:** First professional degree. **Annual earnings:** $113,240. **Annual openings:** 24,040. **Job growth through 2018:** 13.0%.

13. Manufacturing

Education/Training Usually Required: On-the-Job Training or Work Experience

Assemblers and Fabricators

Assemble both finished products and the pieces that go into them, using tools, machines, and hands. **Skill levels:** *Medium:* Mechanical. *Low:* Managerial, mathematics, science. **Education and training:** Short-term on-the-job training; moderate-term on-the-job training. **Annual earnings:** $28,323. **Annual openings:** 42,580. **Job growth through 2018:** −1.9%.

Camera and Photographic Equipment Repairers

Repair and adjust cameras and photographic equipment, including commercial video and motion picture camera equipment. **Skill levels:** *High:* Mechanical, science. *Medium:* Artistic, managerial. *Low:* Communication, interpersonal, mathematics.

Education and training: Long-term on-the-job training. **Annual earnings:** $35,420. **Annual openings:** 130. **Job growth through 2018:** –15.4%.

Computer Control Programmers and Operators

Operate or develop programs for computer-controlled machines or robots to perform one or more machine functions on metal or plastic work pieces. **Skill levels:** *High:* Mathematics, mechanical. *Medium:* Science. *Low:* Managerial. **Education and training:** Moderate-term on-the-job training; work experience in a related occupation. **Annual earnings:** $35,691. **Annual openings:** 4,020. **Job growth through 2018:** 4.3%.

Elevator Installers and Repairers

Assemble, install, repair, or maintain electric or hydraulic freight or passenger elevators, escalators, or dumbwaiters. **Skill levels:** *High:* Mathematics, mechanical, science. *Medium:* Communication, managerial. *Low:* Artistic, interpersonal. **Education and training:** Long-term on-the-job training. **Annual earnings:** $69,050. **Annual openings:** 920. **Job growth through 2018:** 9.2%.

Heavy Vehicle and Mobile Equipment Service Technicians and Mechanics

Repair and maintain engines and hydraulic, transmission, and electrical systems for equipment used in industrial activities such as construction and railroad transportation. **Skill levels:** *High:* Mechanical. *Medium:* Science. *Low:* Interpersonal, managerial, mathematics. **Education and training:** Long-term on-the-job training. **Annual earnings:** $42,440. **Annual openings:** 5,170. **Job growth through 2018:** 8.1%.

Industrial Machinery Mechanics and Millwrights

Assemble, set up, maintain, and repair machines that produce power or manufacture products. **Skill levels:** *High:* Mathematics, mechanical, science. *Low:* Artistic, interpersonal, managerial. **Education and training:** Moderate-term on-the-job training; long-term on-the-job training. **Annual earnings:** $43,707. **Annual openings:** 8,730. **Job growth through 2018:** 6.1%.

Inspectors, Testers, Sorters, Samplers, and Weighers

Inspect, test, sort, sample, or weigh nonagricultural raw materials or processed, machined, fabricated, or assembled parts or products for defects, wear, and deviations from specifications. **Skill levels:** *Medium:* Mathematics, mechanical, science. *Low:* Communication. **Education and training:** Moderate-term on-the-job training. **Annual earnings:** $32,330. **Annual openings:** 7,790. **Job growth through 2018:** –3.6%.

Machine Setters, Operators, and Tenders—Metal and Plastic

Set up, operate, or tend machines that process or shape thermoplastic or metal materials. **Skill levels:** *High:* Mechanical. *Medium:* Science. *Low:* Mathematics. **Education and training:** Moderate-term on-the-job training; long-term on-the-job training. **Annual earnings:** $30,930. **Annual openings:** 19,910. **Job growth through 2018:** −12.6%.

Machinists

Set up and operate a variety of machine tools to produce precision parts and instruments. **Skill levels:** *High:* Mechanical. *Medium:* Artistic. *Low:* Mathematics. **Education and training:** Long-term on-the-job training. **Annual earnings:** $37,650. **Annual openings:** 5,560. **Job growth through 2018:** −4.6%.

Material Moving Occupations

Operate machines or use hand labor to move materials such as freight, parts in a production process, liquids or gases in a pipeline, or construction materials. **Skill levels:** *Medium:* Mechanical. *Low:* Science. **Education and training:** Short-term on-the-job training; moderate-term on-the-job training; long-term on-the-job training. **Annual earnings:** $24,223. **Annual openings:** 135,720. **Job growth through 2018:** −1.0%.

Musical Instrument Repairers and Tuners

Repair percussion, stringed, reed, or wind instruments. **Skill levels:** *High:* Artistic, managerial, mechanical. *Medium:* Mathematics, science. *Low:* Communication. **Education and training:** Long-term on-the-job training. **Annual earnings:** $32,800. **Annual openings:** 180. **Job growth through 2018:** 0.0%.

Painting and Coating Workers, Except Construction and Maintenance

Apply coating or paint by machine or by hand to any of various products, including food, glassware, cloth, ceramics, metal, plastic, paper, or wood; materials applied may be lacquer, silver, copper, rubber, varnish, glaze, enamel, oil, or rust-proofing materials. **Skill levels:** *Medium:* Artistic, mechanical, science. *Low:* Managerial, mathematics. **Education and training:** Short-term on-the-job training; moderate-term on-the-job training. **Annual earnings:** $30,853. **Annual openings:** 5,780. **Job growth through 2018:** 3.8%.

Power Plant Operators, Distributors, and Dispatchers

Control the production and distribution of electric power. **Skill levels:** *High:* Mechanical, science. *Medium:* Communication, interpersonal, managerial, mathematics. **Education and training:** Long-term on-the-job training. **Annual earnings:** $62,821. **Annual openings:** 1,840. **Job growth through 2018:** 0.4%.

Sheet Metal Workers

Fabricate, assemble, install, and repair sheet metal products and equipment, such as ducts, control boxes, drainpipes, and furnace casings. **Skill levels:** *High:* Mathematics, mechanical. *Medium:* Science. *Low:* Artistic, communication, interpersonal. **Education and training:** Long-term on-the-job training. **Annual earnings:** $40,640. **Annual openings:** 5,170. **Job growth through 2018:** 6.5%.

Stationary Engineers and Boiler Operators

Operate or maintain stationary engines, boilers, or other mechanical equipment to provide utilities for buildings or industrial processes. **Skill levels:** *High:* Mechanical, science. *Medium:* Interpersonal, managerial, mathematics. *Low:* Communication. **Education and training:** Long-term on-the-job training. **Annual earnings:** $51,370. **Annual openings:** 920. **Job growth through 2018:** 5.2%.

Textile, Apparel, and Furnishings Occupations

Produce fibers, cloth, and upholstery and fashion them into a wide range of products. **Skill levels:** *Medium:* Artistic, mechanical. *Low:* Science. **Education and training:** Short-term on-the-job training; moderate-term on-the-job training; long-term on-the-job training. **Annual earnings:** $21,894. **Annual openings:** 9,550. **Job growth through 2018:** –15.2%.

Tool and Die Makers

Analyze specifications; lay out metal stock; set up and operate machine tools; and fit and assemble parts to make and repair dies, cutting tools, jigs, fixtures, gauges, and machinists' hand tools. **Skill levels:** *High:* Mathematics, mechanical. *Medium:* Artistic, science. **Education and training:** Long-term on-the-job training. **Annual earnings:** $46,900. **Annual openings:** 510. **Job growth through 2018:** –8.0%.

Watch Repairers

Repair, clean, and adjust mechanisms of timing instruments, such as watches and clocks. **Skill levels:** *High:* Mathematics, mechanical, science. *Medium:* Managerial. *Low:* Artistic, communication. **Education and training:** Long-term on-the-job training. **Annual earnings:** $37,680. **Annual openings:** 90. **Job growth through 2018:** –13.8%.

Woodworkers

Design, produce, and test products made from wood, such as furniture, kitchen cabinets, and musical instruments. **Skill levels:** *Medium:* Artistic, mechanical. *Low:* Mathematics. **Education and training:** Moderate-term on-the-job training; long-term on-the-job training. **Annual earnings:** $27,398. **Annual openings:** 8,930. **Job growth through 2018:** 6.4%.

Education/Training Usually Required: Postsecondary, Less Than Four Years

Computer, Automated Teller, and Office Machine Repairers

Repair, maintain, or install computers, word-processing systems, automated teller machines, and electronic office machines, such as duplicating and fax machines. **Skill levels:** *High:* Mechanical, science. *Medium:* Communication, interpersonal, managerial, mathematics. *Low:* Artistic. **Education and training:** Postsecondary vocational training. **Annual earnings:** $37,620. **Annual openings:** 2,630. **Job growth through 2018:** –4.4%.

Electrical and Electronics Installers and Repairers

Install, maintain, and repair complex electronic equipment and electrical systems. **Skill levels:** *High:* Mathematics, mechanical, science. *Medium:* Artistic. *Low:* Communication, interpersonal, managerial. **Education and training:** Postsecondary vocational training. **Annual earnings:** $47,397. **Annual openings:** 3,930. **Job growth through 2018:** 4.7%.

Jewelers and Precious Stone and Metal Workers

Design, fabricate, adjust, repair, or appraise jewelry, gold, silver, other precious metals, or gems. **Skill levels:** *Medium:* Artistic, managerial, mathematics, mechanical, science. *Low:* Interpersonal. **Education and training:** Postsecondary vocational training. **Annual earnings:** $34,060. **Annual openings:** 1,350. **Job growth through 2018:** 5.3%.

Medical Equipment Repairers

Test, adjust, or repair biomedical or electromedical equipment. **Skill levels:** *High:* Mathematics, mechanical, science. *Medium:* Communication, interpersonal, managerial. *Low:* Artistic. **Education and training:** Associate degree. **Annual earnings:** $42,300. **Annual openings:** 2,320. **Job growth through 2018:** 27.2%.

Semiconductor Processors

Perform any or all of the following functions in the manufacture of electronic semiconductors: load semiconductor material into furnace; saw formed ingots into segments; load individual segment into crystal growing chamber and monitor controls; locate crystal axis in ingot, using X-ray equipment, and saw ingots into wafers; clean, polish, and load wafers into series of special-purpose furnaces, chemical baths, and equipment used to form circuitry and change conductive properties. **Skill levels:** *High:* Mechanical. *Medium:* Science. *Low:* Artistic, interpersonal, managerial, mathematics. **Education and training:** Postsecondary vocational training. **Annual earnings:** $31,570. **Annual openings:** 650. **Job growth through 2018:** –31.5%.

Welding, Soldering, and Brazing Workers

Use molten metal to join metal parts or to fill holes, indentations, or seams of metal products. **Skill levels:** *Medium:* Mechanical, science. *Low:* Mathematics. **Education and training:** Postsecondary vocational training. **Annual earnings:** $34,542. **Annual openings:** 14,290. **Job growth through 2018:** –2.3%.

Education/Training Usually Required: Bachelor's Degree or Higher

No occupations at this level.

14. Retail and Wholesale Sales and Service

Education/Training Usually Required: On-the-Job Training or Work Experience

Cashiers

Receive and disburse money in establishments other than financial institutions. **Skill levels:** *Low:* Artistic, mechanical. **Education and training:** Short-term on-the-job training. **Annual earnings:** $17,820. **Annual openings:** 171,990. **Job growth through 2018:** 3.5%.

Counter and Rental Clerks

Receive orders for repairs, rentals, and services. **Skill levels:** *Low:* Artistic, mechanical. **Education and training:** Short-term on-the-job training. **Annual earnings:** $21,300. **Annual openings:** 13,350. **Job growth through 2018:** 3.1%.

Demonstrators and Product Promoters

Demonstrate merchandise and answer questions for the purpose of creating public interest in buying the product. **Skill levels:** *Medium:* Artistic. *Low:* Communication, interpersonal, managerial, mathematics, mechanical, science. **Education and training:** Moderate-term on-the-job training. **Annual earnings:** $22,510. **Annual openings:** 3,690. **Job growth through 2018:** 7.1%.

Gaming Cage Workers

In a gaming establishment, conduct financial transactions for patrons. **Skill levels:** *Low:* Mathematics, mechanical. **Education and training:** Short-term on-the-job training. **Annual earnings:** $23,464. **Annual openings:** 1,320. **Job growth through 2018:** –10.4%.

Hotel, Motel, and Resort Desk Clerks

Accommodate hotel, motel, and resort patrons by registering and assigning rooms to guests, issuing room keys, transmitting and receiving messages, keeping records of occupied rooms and guests' accounts, making and confirming reservations, and presenting statements to and collecting payments from departing guests. **Skill levels:** *Low:* Artistic, communication, interpersonal, mathematics, mechanical, science. **Education and training:** Short-term on-the-job training. **Annual earnings:** $19,820. **Annual openings:** 10,950. **Job growth through 2018:** 13.7%.

Models

Model garments and other apparel to display clothing before prospective buyers at fashion shows, private showings, retail establishments, or photographer. **Skill levels:** *High:* Artistic. **Education and training:** Moderate-term on-the-job training. **Annual earnings:** $27,330. **Annual openings:** 100. **Job growth through 2018:** 16.1%.

Purchasing Managers, Buyers, and Purchasing Agents

Buy a vast array of farm products, durable and nondurable goods, and services for companies and institutions. **Skill levels:** *High:* Managerial, mathematics. *Medium:* Communication, interpersonal, mechanical. *Low:* Science. **Education and training:** Long-term on-the-job training; work experience plus degree. **Annual earnings:** $58,268. **Annual openings:** 17,980. **Job growth through 2018:** 7.3%.

Real Estate Brokers and Sales Agents

Help people who are buying or selling real estate. **Skill levels:** *High:* Interpersonal. *Medium:* Communication, managerial, mathematics. *Low:* Artistic, science. **Education and training:** Work experience in a related occupation; postsecondary vocational training. **Annual earnings:** $43,885. **Annual openings:** 15,910. **Job growth through 2018:** 14.4%.

Retail Salespersons

Sell merchandise such as furniture, motor vehicles, appliances, or apparel in a retail establishment. **Skill levels:** *Low:* Artistic, communication, mathematics. **Education and training:** Short-term on-the-job training. **Annual earnings:** $20,260. **Annual openings:** 162,690. **Job growth through 2018:** 8.3%.

Sales Representatives, Wholesale and Manufacturing

Make customers interested in manufacturers' and wholesalers' merchandise and arrange the sale of that merchandise. **Skill levels:** *High:* Interpersonal, managerial. *Medium:* Communication, mathematics, science. *Low:* Mechanical. **Education and training:** Work experience in a related occupation. **Annual earnings:** $55,487. **Annual openings:** 60,020. **Job growth through 2018:** 7.3%.

Sales Worker Supervisors

Oversee the work of sales and related workers, such as retail salespersons, cashiers, customer service representatives, stock clerks and order fillers, sales engineers, and wholesale sales representatives. **Skill levels:** *High:* Managerial. *Medium:* Communication, interpersonal, mathematics, mechanical. *Low:* Artistic, science. **Education and training:** Work experience in a related occupation. **Annual earnings:** $40,873. **Annual openings:** 57,960. **Job growth through 2018:** 5.1%.

Stock Clerks and Order Fillers

Receive, store, and issue sales floor merchandise, materials, equipment, and other items from stockroom, warehouse, or storage yard to fill shelves, racks, tables, or customers' orders. **Skill levels:** *Low:* Mathematics, mechanical. **Education and training:** Short-term on-the-job training. **Annual earnings:** $20,960. **Annual openings:** 56,260. **Job growth through 2018:** 7.2%.

Education/Training Usually Required: Postsecondary, Less Than Four Years

Appraisers and Assessors of Real Estate

Appraise real property to determine its fair value. **Skill levels:** *High:* Mathematics. *Medium:* Communication, interpersonal, managerial. *Low:* Mechanical, science. **Education and training:** Associate degree. **Annual earnings:** $47,840. **Annual openings:** 2,100. **Job growth through 2018:** 4.6%.

Real Estate Brokers and Sales Agents

Help people who are buying or selling real estate. **Skill levels:** *High:* Interpersonal. *Medium:* Communication, managerial, mathematics. *Low:* Artistic, science. **Education and training:** Work experience in a related occupation; postsecondary vocational training. **Annual earnings:** $43,885. **Annual openings:** 15,910. **Job growth through 2018:** 14.4%.

Education/Training Usually Required: Bachelor's Degree or Higher

Advertising, Marketing, Promotions, Public Relations, and Sales Managers

Coordinate their companies' market research, marketing strategy, sales, advertising, promotion, pricing, product development, and public relations activities. **Skill levels:** *High:* Interpersonal, managerial. *Medium:* Artistic, communication. *Low:* Mathematics. **Education and training:** Work experience plus degree. **Annual earnings:** $99,085. **Annual openings:** 21,740. **Job growth through 2018:** 12.9%.

Market and Survey Researchers

Gather information about people's preferences and opinions for companies, governments, and other organizations. **Skill levels:** *High:* Communication, interpersonal. *Medium:* Artistic, managerial, science. *Low:* Mathematics. **Education and training:** Bachelor's degree. **Annual earnings:** $59,424. **Annual openings:** 15,070. **Job growth through 2018:** 28.3%.

Meeting and Convention Planners

Coordinate activities of staff and convention personnel to make arrangements for group meetings and conventions. **Skill levels:** *Medium:* Artistic, interpersonal, managerial. *Low:* Communication. **Education and training:** Bachelor's degree. **Annual earnings:** $44,780. **Annual openings:** 2,140. **Job growth through 2018:** 15.6%.

Property, Real Estate, and Community Association Managers

Plan, direct, or coordinate selling, buying, leasing, or governance activities of commercial, industrial, or residential real estate properties. **Skill levels:** *High:* Managerial. *Medium:* Interpersonal, mathematics, mechanical. *Low:* Artistic, communication, science. **Education and training:** Bachelor's degree. **Annual earnings:** $48,460. **Annual openings:** 7,800. **Job growth through 2018:** 8.4%.

Purchasing Managers, Buyers, and Purchasing Agents

Buy a vast array of farm products, durable and nondurable goods, and services for companies and institutions. **Skill levels:** *High:* Managerial, mathematics. *Medium:* Communication, interpersonal, mechanical. *Low:* Science. **Education and training:** Long-term on-the-job training; work experience plus degree. **Annual earnings:** $58,268. **Annual openings:** 17,980. **Job growth through 2018:** 7.3%.

Sales Engineers

Sell business goods or services, the selling of which requires a technical background equivalent to a baccalaureate degree in engineering. **Skill levels:** *High:* Communication, interpersonal, managerial, mathematics, mechanical, science. *Medium:* Artistic. **Education and training:** Bachelor's degree. **Annual earnings:** $83,190. **Annual openings:** 3,500. **Job growth through 2018:** 8.8%.

15. Scientific Research, Engineering, and Mathematics

Education/Training Usually Required: On-the-Job Training or Work Experience

No occupations at this level.

Education/Training Usually Required: Postsecondary, Less Than Four Years

Engineering Technicians

Use the principles and theories of science, engineering, and mathematics to solve technical problems in research and development, manufacturing, sales, construction, inspection, and maintenance. **Skill levels:** *High:* Mathematics, mechanical. *Medium:* Artistic, communication, science. *Low:* Interpersonal, managerial. **Education and training:** Associate degree. **Annual earnings:** $51,174. **Annual openings:** 12,480. **Job growth through 2018:** 5.2%.

Occupational Health and Safety Technicians

Collect data on work environments for analysis by occupational health and safety specialists. **Skill levels:** *High:* Communication, interpersonal, managerial, mathematics, science. *Medium:* Mechanical. *Low:* Artistic. **Education and training:** Associate degree. **Annual earnings:** $44,830. **Annual openings:** 520. **Job growth through 2018:** 14.5%.

Science Technicians

Assist scientists by using principles and theories of science and mathematics to solve problems in research and development and to help invent and improve products and processes. **Skill levels:** *High:* Mathematics, mechanical, science. *Medium:* Communication, managerial. *Low:* Artistic, interpersonal. **Education and training:**

Associate degree; bachelor's degree. **Annual earnings:** $40,963. **Annual openings:** 12,380. **Job growth through 2018:** 11.7%.

Education/Training Usually Required: Bachelor's Degree or Higher

Archivists, Curators, and Museum Technicians

Work for museums, governments, zoos, colleges and universities, corporations, and other institutions that require experts to preserve important records and artifacts. **Skill levels:** *High:* Communication, managerial. *Medium:* Artistic, interpersonal, mathematics, mechanical, science. **Education and training:** Bachelor's degree; master's degree. **Annual earnings:** $43,335. **Annual openings:** 1,460. **Job growth through 2018:** 20.4%.

Atmospheric Scientists

Study the atmosphere's physical characteristics, motions, and processes and the way in which these factors affect the rest of our environment. **Skill levels:** *High:* Communication, interpersonal, mathematics, science. *Medium:* Artistic, managerial, mechanical. **Education and training:** Bachelor's degree. **Annual earnings:** $84,710. **Annual openings:** 330. **Job growth through 2018:** 14.6%.

Biological Scientists

Study living organisms and their relationship to the environment to gain a better understanding of fundamental life processes or apply that understanding to developing new products or processes. **Skill levels:** *High:* Communication, managerial, mathematics, science. *Medium:* Artistic, interpersonal. *Low:* Mechanical. **Education and training:** Bachelor's degree; doctoral degree. **Annual earnings:** $68,707. **Annual openings:** 4,860. **Job growth through 2018:** 21.0%.

Chemists and Materials Scientists

Conduct chemical analyses or chemical experiments in laboratories for quality or process control or to develop new products or knowledge. **Skill levels:** *High:* Communication, interpersonal, managerial, mathematics, mechanical, science. *Medium:* Artistic. **Education and training:** Bachelor's degree. **Annual earnings:** $69,428. **Annual openings:** 3,440. **Job growth through 2018:** 3.5%.

Economists

Conduct research, prepare reports, or formulate plans to aid in solution of economic problems arising from production and distribution of goods and services. **Skill levels:** *High:* Communication, interpersonal, mathematics. *Medium:* Artistic, managerial, science. *Low:* Mechanical. **Education and training:** Master's degree. **Annual earnings:** $86,930. **Annual openings:** 500. **Job growth through 2018:** 5.8%.

Engineering and Natural Sciences Managers

Plan, coordinate, and direct research, design, and production activities. **Skill levels:** *High:* Managerial, mathematics. *Medium:* Artistic, communication, interpersonal, science. **Education and training:** Work experience plus degree. **Annual earnings:** $116,515. **Annual openings:** 6,880. **Job growth through 2018:** 8.0%.

Engineers

Use scientific and mathematical principles to create products, improve processes, and solve problems. **Skill levels:** *High:* Communication, interpersonal, managerial, mathematics, science. *Medium:* Artistic, mechanical. **Education and training:** Bachelor's degree. **Annual earnings:** $82,632. **Annual openings:** 53,170. **Job growth through 2018:** 11.3%.

Epidemiologists

Investigate and describe the determinants and distribution of disease, disability, and other health outcomes and develop the means for prevention and control. **Skill levels:** *Medium:* Communication, managerial, mathematics, science. *Low:* Artistic, interpersonal. **Education and training:** Master's degree. **Annual earnings:** $61,700. **Annual openings:** 170. **Job growth through 2018:** 15.1%.

Geoscientists and Hydrologists

Study the composition, structure, and other physical aspects of the Earth and the Earth's geologic past and present by using sophisticated instruments to analyze the composition of earth, rock, and water. **Skill levels:** *High:* Science. *Medium:* Artistic, communication, mathematics. *Low:* Interpersonal, managerial. **Education and training:** Master's degree. **Annual earnings:** $79,836. **Annual openings:** 1,920. **Job growth through 2018:** 17.7%.

Mathematicians

Use mathematical theory and techniques to solve economic, scientific, engineering, physics, and business problems. **Skill levels:** *High:* Artistic, communication, mathematics, science. *Low:* Interpersonal, managerial, mechanical. **Education and training:** Doctoral degree. **Annual earnings:** $93,580. **Annual openings:** 150. **Job growth through 2018:** 22.4%.

Medical Scientists

Research human diseases to improve human health. **Skill levels:** *High:* Artistic, communication, interpersonal, managerial, mathematics, science. *Medium:* Mechanical. **Education and training:** Doctoral degree. **Annual earnings:** $74,590. **Annual openings:** 6,620. **Job growth through 2018:** 40.4%.

Operations Research Analysts

Assist managers with decision making, policy formulation, or other managerial functions by creating and applying mathematical models and other optimizing methods. **Skill levels:** *High:* Communication, managerial, mathematics, science. *Medium:* Artistic, interpersonal. *Low:* Mechanical. **Education and training:** Master's degree. **Annual earnings:** $70,070. **Annual openings:** 3,220. **Job growth through 2018:** 22.0%.

Physicists and Astronomers

Conduct research to understand the nature of the universe and everything in it. **Skill levels:** *High:* Communication, interpersonal, managerial, mathematics, science. *Medium:* Artistic, mechanical. **Education and training:** Doctoral degree. **Annual earnings:** $106,251. **Annual openings:** 760. **Job growth through 2018:** 15.9%.

Science Technicians

Assist scientists by using principles and theories of science and mathematics to solve problems in research and development and to help invent and improve products and processes. **Skill levels:** *High:* Mathematics, mechanical, science. *Medium:* Communication, managerial. *Low:* Artistic, interpersonal. **Education and training:** Associate degree; bachelor's degree. **Annual earnings:** $40,963. **Annual openings:** 12,380. **Job growth through 2018:** 11.7%.

Social Scientists, Other

Research, analyze, and report on all aspects of human society. **Skill levels:** *High:* Artistic, communication, interpersonal, managerial, science. *Medium:* Mathematics. *Low:* Mechanical. **Education and training:** Master's degree. **Annual earnings:** $54,652. **Annual openings:** 800. **Job growth through 2018:** 21.7%.

Sociologists and Political Scientists

Study all aspects of human society and political systems—from social behavior and the origin of social groups to the origin, development, and operation of political systems. **Skill levels:** *High:* Artistic, communication, interpersonal, managerial, mathematics, science. **Education and training:** Master's degree. **Annual earnings:** $85,911. **Annual openings:** 480. **Job growth through 2018:** 20.8%.

Statisticians

Engage in the development of mathematical theory or apply statistical theory and methods to collect, organize, interpret, and summarize numerical data to provide usable information. **Skill levels:** *High:* Communication, interpersonal, mathematics, science. *Medium:* Artistic, managerial. *Low:* Mechanical. **Education and training:** Master's degree. **Annual earnings:** $72,820. **Annual openings:** 960. **Job growth through 2018:** 13.1%.

16. Transportation, Distribution, and Logistics

Education/Training Usually Required: On-the-Job Training or Work Experience

Air Traffic Controllers

Control air traffic on and within vicinity of airport and movement of air traffic between altitude sectors and control centers according to established procedures and policies. **Skill levels:** *High:* Science. *Medium:* Communication, interpersonal, mathematics, mechanical. *Low:* Managerial. **Education and training:** Long-term on-the-job training. **Annual earnings:** $109,850. **Annual openings:** 1,230. **Job growth through 2018:** 13.1%.

Automotive Body and Related Repairers

Repair and refinish automotive vehicle bodies and straighten vehicle frames. **Skill levels:** *High:* Mechanical. *Medium:* Science. *Low:* Artistic, managerial, mathematics. **Education and training:** Long-term on-the-job training. **Annual earnings:** $37,458. **Annual openings:** 4,820. **Job growth through 2018:** 0.6%.

Bus Drivers

Drive bus or motor coach, including regular route operations, charters, and private carriage, serving passengers such as commuters, schoolchildren, and vacationers. **Skill levels:** *Medium:* Interpersonal, mechanical. *Low:* Science. **Education and training:** Moderate-term on-the-job training. **Annual earnings:** $29,289. **Annual openings:** 15,700. **Job growth through 2018:** 6.8%.

Flight Attendants

Provide personal services to ensure the safety and comfort of airline passengers during flight. **Skill levels:** *Medium:* Artistic, interpersonal. *Low:* Communication, mechanical. **Education and training:** Long-term on-the-job training. **Annual earnings:** $40,010. **Annual openings:** 3,010. **Job growth through 2018:** 8.1%.

Production, Planning, and Expediting Clerks

Coordinate and expedite the flow of work and materials within or between departments of an establishment according to production schedule. **Skill levels:** *High:* Interpersonal, managerial, mathematics. *Medium:* Communication, science. *Low:* Mechanical. **Education and training:** Moderate-term on-the-job training. **Annual earnings:** $41,560. **Annual openings:** 7,410. **Job growth through 2018:** 1.5%.

Rail Transportation Occupations

Perform various functions for one of the three types of railroads: freight, passenger, or urban transit (subway and light rail). **Skill levels:** *Medium:* Mechanical. *Low:* Communication, science. **Education and training:** Moderate-term on-the-job training. **Annual earnings:** $49,537. **Annual openings:** 3,340. **Job growth through 2018:** 8.7%.

Shipping, Receiving, and Traffic Clerks

Verify and keep records on incoming and outgoing shipments. **Skill levels:** *High:* Mathematics. *Medium:* Communication, managerial, science. *Low:* Interpersonal, mechanical. **Education and training:** Short-term on-the-job training. **Annual earnings:** $28,250. **Annual openings:** 18,620. **Job growth through 2018:** –6.6%.

Small Engine Mechanics

Diagnose, adjust, repair, or overhaul small engines used to power lawn mowers, chain saws, and related equipment. **Skill levels:** *High:* Mechanical, science. *Medium:* Mathematics. *Low:* Communication, managerial. **Education and training:** Moderate-term on-the-job training; long-term on-the-job training. **Annual earnings:** $31,813. **Annual openings:** 1,940. **Job growth through 2018:** 6.8%.

Taxi Drivers and Chauffeurs

Drive automobiles, vans, or limousines to transport passengers. **Skill levels:** *Medium:* Mechanical. **Education and training:** Short-term on-the-job training. **Annual earnings:** $21,960. **Annual openings:** 7,730. **Job growth through 2018:** 15.5%.

Truck Drivers and Driver/Sales Workers

Drive truck or other vehicle to pick up and deliver freight or other goods or to sell goods, such as food products, over an established route. **Skill levels:** *High:* Mechanical. *Low:* Interpersonal, mathematics, science. **Education and training:** Short-term on-the-job training. **Annual earnings:** $32,895. **Annual openings:** 86,250. **Job growth through 2018:** 9.2%.

Water Transportation Occupations

Operate and maintain civilian-owned deep-sea merchant ships, tugboats, towboats, ferries, barges, offshore supply vessels, cruise ships, and other waterborne craft on the oceans, the Great Lakes, rivers, canals, and other waterways, as well as in harbors. **Skill levels:** *High:* Mechanical. *Medium:* Science. *Low:* Communication, interpersonal, managerial, mathematics. **Education and training:** Short-term on-the-job training; moderate-term on-the-job training; work experience in a related occupation. **Annual earnings:** $51,003. **Annual openings:** 4,620. **Job growth through 2018:** 14.8%.

Education/Training Usually Required: Postsecondary, Less Than Four Years

Aircraft and Avionics Equipment Mechanics and Service Technicians

Perform scheduled maintenance, make repairs, and complete inspections on airplanes according to FAA requirements. **Skill levels:** *High:* Mechanical. *Medium:* Communication, mathematics. *Low:* Artistic, managerial, science. **Education and training:** Postsecondary vocational training. **Annual earnings:** $52,501. **Annual openings:** 3,660. **Job growth through 2018:** 7.0%.

Aircraft Pilots and Flight Engineers

Fly airplanes or helicopters to carry out a wide variety of tasks, including transporting passengers and cargo, dusting crops, spreading seed for reforestation, testing aircraft, directing firefighting efforts, tracking criminals, monitoring traffic, and rescuing and evacuating injured persons. **Skill levels:** *High:* Communication, interpersonal, mathematics, mechanical, science. *Medium:* Managerial. **Education and training:** Postsecondary vocational training; bachelor's degree. **Annual earnings:** $94,861. **Annual openings:** 5,310. **Job growth through 2018:** 11.8%.

Automotive Service Technicians and Mechanics

Diagnose, adjust, repair, or overhaul automotive vehicles. **Skill levels:** *High:* Mechanical. *Medium:* Mathematics, science. *Low:* Communication, interpersonal, managerial. **Education and training:** Postsecondary vocational training. **Annual earnings:** $35,420. **Annual openings:** 18,170. **Job growth through 2018:** 4.7%.

Diesel Service Technicians and Mechanics

Repair and maintain the diesel engines that power equipment for transportation and other purposes. **Skill levels:** *High:* Mechanical. *Medium:* Science. *Low:* Interpersonal, managerial. **Education and training:** Postsecondary vocational training. **Annual earnings:** $40,250. **Annual openings:** 7,530. **Job growth through 2018:** 5.7%.

Education/Training Usually Required: Bachelor's Degree or Higher

Aircraft Pilots and Flight Engineers

Fly airplanes or helicopters to carry out a wide variety of tasks, including transporting passengers and cargo, dusting crops, spreading seed for reforestation, testing aircraft, directing firefighting efforts, tracking criminals, monitoring traffic, and rescuing and evacuating injured persons. **Skill levels:** *High:* Communication, interpersonal, mathematics, mechanical, science. *Medium:* Managerial. **Education and training:** Postsecondary vocational training; bachelor's degree. **Annual earnings:** $94,861. **Annual openings:** 5,310. **Job growth through 2018:** 11.8%.

Go Back and Review the Job Descriptions

Go back to the jobs you checked and read their descriptions to learn more about them. This step will help you eliminate some jobs and identify the relatively few jobs that are *most* interesting to you. Circle or underline the relatively few jobs that interest you most. When you are done, write the five to ten jobs that most interest you in the box that follows. Do not eliminate any job that interests you because of its education requirements, skills, or other factors. If it interests you and you think you would enjoy it, list the job in the following box. You can always eliminate it later.

MY TOP JOB TITLES
1. _____
2. _____
3. _____
4. _____
5. _____
6. _____
7. _____
8. _____
9. _____
10. _____

You will need to learn more about some of the jobs on your list before making a final decision. Some may require additional training or education, for example.

The Job Exploration Worksheet in Appendix A can help you do more research on specific jobs as needed. In Chapter 8, you will combine your top job titles with your career preferences from earlier chapters to create your career focus.

More About the Data in the Job Descriptions

Here are more details on the information in the job descriptions.

Understanding the Skill Levels

For each description, from one to seven skills are listed and rated as high, medium, or low. High skill levels are essential to the job. Medium skill levels are important but not essential. Low-level skills are mildly important for the job. The skill information was derived from the O*NET database of the U.S. Department of Labor.

Occupations are assigned skills based on the level of competency that is usually needed. The ratings in the job descriptions are averages, based on tasks that are most commonly performed by the majority of workers in each occupation. For example, a high level of mathematics skills is not required for some computer programmers, such as those who work on user interfaces, but high-level math skills are required for most computer programmers—including some who prepare physics simulations that require calculus. Based on the level of skills that most of these workers need, mathematics ability is rated high, or essential, for computer programmers. In another example, managerial skills are rated as being of low importance for insulation workers, who are primarily independent but sometimes must advise other workers.

Here is some general information about the skills in the job descriptions:

- **Artistic skills:** Occupations that require artistic skills tap workers' sense of what is beautiful, is well designed, has a good appearance, or displays a visual pattern.

- **Communication skills:** Nearly all workers need communication skills. But the job descriptions show which occupations require more complex levels of English language comprehension.

- **Interpersonal skills:** Interpersonal skills refer to workers' ability to interact effectively with other people and to be persuasive.

- **Managerial skills:** Managerial skills include the ability to organize, direct, and instruct other workers and manage time and resources.

- **Mathematics skills:** Mathematics skills refer to more advanced ability than the core math skills required in nearly all jobs. The rating shows either the frequency or complexity of the skill required.

- **Mechanical skills:** Mechanical skills include a broad range of abilities, such as installation, maintenance, troubleshooting, and quality control analysis.

- **Science skills:** Basic science skills include an ability to apply some scientific theories and to communicate about science. Moderate science skills involve theoretical scientific knowledge, and high-level science skills involve in-depth practical knowledge.

Understanding the Education Levels

This "education and training" entry in the job descriptions gives you information on the education and training typically required for entry into the job. Some jobs that interest you may require more training or education than you have or want to consider getting. Don't eliminate these too quickly! If a job really interests you, learn more about it. If you really want to do that kind of work, you can often find ways to get the training or education needed.

Here is more information on the education and training levels used in the job descriptions:

- **First professional degree:** Typically requires a minimum of two years of education beyond the bachelor's degree and frequently requires three years.

- **Doctoral degree:** Normally requires two or more years of full-time academic work beyond the bachelor's degree.

- **Master's degree:** Usually requires one to two years of full-time study beyond the bachelor's degree.

- **Work experience plus degree:** Bachelor's or master's degree plus related work experience. Jobs requiring this education level are often management-related and require some experience in a related non-managerial position.

- **Bachelor's degree:** A four-year academic program beyond high school.

- **Associate degree:** A two-year academic program beyond high school.

- **Postsecondary vocational training:** Specific job-related training lasting from several months to several years. Some high schools provide substantial vocational training, although most is obtained after high school.

- **Work experience in a related occupation:** Experience in a related job.

- **Long-term on-the-job training:** More than one year of on-the-job training or a combination of training and formal classroom instruction.

- **Moderate-term on-the-job training:** One to twelve months of on-the-job training.

- **Short-term on-the-job training:** Up to one month of on-the-job training.

Understanding Earnings, Openings, and Job Growth Information

The average wage for all jobs is $32,390. The average growth for all jobs is 10.1 percent through 2018.

To create the data in the job descriptions, we linked the *Occupational Outlook Handbook* jobs to the latest information on wages, employment outlook, and requirements for education or training from the U.S. Department of Labor. In cases where an *OOH* job is linked to more than one job for which data is gathered (for example, Conservation Scientists and Foresters), we calculated a weighted average for wages and job growth and summed the figures for job openings.

What's Next?

Now that you have identified the job titles that interest you most and the other factors important to you in a career, the next chapter helps you look at the industries you may enjoy.

Key Points: Chapter 6

- Focusing on job titles may cause you to overlook factors that are important for career success.

- Accurate information about specific jobs is a key part of career planning.

- The jobs described in this chapter appear in a longer form in the *Occupational Outlook Handbook,* a book published every two years by the U.S. Department of Labor and available from JIST.

Chapter 7

Identify Industries That Interest You

While most people understand the advantage of wanting a certain type of job rather than "any" job, they often overlook the importance of considering various industries. Yet the industry you work in is often as important as what job you choose. Why? There are various reasons, but here are the primary ones:

- **Some industries pay better.** Let's say you want to manage a warehouse operation or work in an office-support position. If so, it might help you to know that you are more likely to be paid better in the drug manufacturing industry than in the department store or grocery store industries. You have the same basic job, doing the same basic sorts of things, but one industry pays better. That could end up being a very important difference to you over time.

- **Some industries present more risk or less stability.** Some industries routinely hire more people when the economy is strong and lay off people when it is weak. Other industries tend to be more stable in their employment and less affected by short-term business cycles. Some industries are growing rapidly, others are declining, and many are changing as a result of technology or other forces. If it is important for you to work in a stable situation where you are less likely to be laid off, then select a more stable industry.

- **Some industries are a better match for your strongest skills.** In an industry that suits your abilities, employers will be more likely to recognize your potential and achievements will come more easily.

- **Some industries will be more fun for you.** Some industries will appeal to you more for a variety of reasons. You could be interested based on your interests, values, previous training or education, or a variety of other factors. Selecting an industry that appeals to you could be as important to you as the job you do.

Some Background on Industry Growth

The data that follows shows the projected growth in number of people employed in various industries in the ten-year period ending 2018. The table also gives you information on the percent of the total workforce within each industry and industry group.

While this is a lot of data to absorb, it relates to some things you should consider in making your career plans. As you look at the data, notice that it is organized into two major groups consisting of "goods-producing industries" and "service-providing industries." Within these two major groups are subgroups of related industries. Comments and observations on some trends in the industries follow the data table.

Projected Growth by Industry		
Industry	Percent of Workforce Employed	Percent Growth in Employment
ALL INDUSTRIES	**100**	**10.5**
GOODS-PRODUCING INDUSTRIES	**16.7**	**–0.2**
Natural resources, construction, and utilities	**7.1**	**11.9**
Agriculture, forestry, and fishing	0.8	–0.4
Construction	5.6	18.5
Mining	0.4	–14.5
Utilities	0.3	–10.6
Manufacturing	**7.9**	**–9.0**
Aerospace product and parts manufacturing	0.3	–0.3
Chemical manufacturing, except drugs	0.3	–13.3
Computer and electronic product manufacturing	0.7	–19.3
Food manufacturing	1.0	–0.1
Machinery manufacturing	0.7	–7.6
Motor vehicle and parts manufacturing	0.5	–18.3
Pharmaceutical and medicine manufacturing	0.2	6.1
Printing	0.3	–18.0
Steel manufacturing	0.1	–12.7
Textile, textile product, and apparel manufacturing	0.2	–47.9

Industry	Percent of Workforce Employed	Percent Growth in Employment
SERVICE-PRODUCING INDUSTRIES	**78.9**	**12.8**
Trade	**14.5**	**4.3**
Automobile dealers	0.7	−5.7
Clothing, accessory, and general merchandise stores	1.3	11.1
Grocery stores	1.6	0.5
Wholesale trade	4.0	4.3
Transportation and warehousing	**3.2**	**9.9**
Air transportation	0.3	7.5
Truck transportation and warehousing	1.5	11.0
Information	**2.0**	**3.9**
Broadcasting	0.2	7.4
Motion picture and video industries	0.3	14.1
Publishing, except software	0.3	−19.3
Software publishers	0.2	30.0
Telecommunications	0.6	−8.8
Financial activities	**5.7**	**6.8**
Banking	1.3	7.9
Insurance	1.5	2.9
Securities, commodities, and other investments	0.6	11.8
Professional and business services	**14.1**	**23.3**
Advertising and public relations services	0.3	8.0
Computer systems design and related services	1.4	45.3
Employment services	2.4	19.1
Management, scientific, and technical consulting services	1.2	82.8
Scientific research and development services	0.5	25.3
Education, health, and social services	**23.4**	**18.8**
Child day care services	0.6	15.5
Educational services	9.9	12.5
Health care	11.4	22.5

(continued)

(continued)

Industry	Percent of Workforce Employed	Percent Growth in Employment
Social assistance, except child day care	1.5	40.1
Leisure and hospitality	**9.0**	**8.5**
Arts, entertainment, and recreation	1.5	15.5
Food services and drinking places	6.7	7.7
Hotels and other accommodations	1.3	5.4
Government and advocacy, grantmaking, and civic organizations	**8.2**	**9.2**
Advocacy, grantmaking, and civic organizations	1.0	14.1
Federal government	1.4	9.5
State and local government, except education and health	5.8	8.4

Note: May not add to totals due to smaller industries not listed.

This table shows some important things for you to consider in your career planning. Here are some highlights:

Goods-producing industries: These industries manufacture, grow, build, mine, or generate something. Goods-producing industries are projected to decrease slightly, especially in manufacturing. Construction and pharmaceutical and medicine manufacturing are the only specific industries that will see increases.

> **Tip:** *Health services and educational services—the two largest industries—will account for the most new jobs through 2018.*

Service-providing industries: Almost 80 percent of all employment is in this major sector, and this is where much of the future growth is projected to occur. Only three specific industries are expected to decline: automobile dealers, publishing (except software), and telecommunications. All other industries in this large group are expected to increase their employment. As you look through the list, note that some industries are growing much more rapidly than average. Management, scientific, and technical consulting services (82.8 percent); computer systems design and related services (45.3 percent); social assistance, except child day care (40.1 percent); and software publishers (30.0 percent) are among the most rapidly growing industries.

Service-Providing Industries Have Accounted for Virtually All Growth

While recent figures on the increase or decline in industries or occupations seem minor, the information can be quite significant over a long period. Before the industrial revolution, for example, more than 50 percent of the workforce in this country worked on farms. Now, less than 1 percent of our workforce is involved in farming. Something similar has happened more recently with manufacturing. In this case, however, the jobs were lost not to improved technology but to foreign workers. Take a stroll through a big-box store and see how many products you can find that were manufactured in America; unless you're in the food aisle or at the pharmacy, you won't find many.

Most of the growth in employment over recent decades has been in the service-providing industries and not in the goods-producing industries. These services range from high-skill tasks such as managing computer networks, writing legal briefs, and diagnosing illnesses to low-skill tasks such as changing linens in hotel rooms, driving school buses, and flipping burgers.

Keep in mind that opportunities will remain in all industries, including manufacturing, agriculture, and other slow-growth or no-growth industries. This is a very large country, and even small industries that are declining will have openings for well-trained people. What is clear, however, is that this is not your grandparents' economy. Almost all of the net new jobs have been created outside of manufacturing, and this trend is likely to increase.

Most Job Opportunities Are with Small Employers

Many people making career plans think in terms of the biggest companies located in their community. That's where the jobs are, right?

Actually, large employers (businesses that employ more than 500 workers) and small employers each account for about 60 million workers. And it's especially striking to look at large and small *establishments*. Some small businesses, such as a family-owned pizza shop, are located in a single establishment. Other businesses, such as shoe-store chains, are so large that they employ thousands of workers, but the workers are located in many small establishments.

The following table, from the U.S. Department of Labor's *Career Guide to Industries*, shows the percentage of all workers employed in establishments of different sizes. These figures (from March 2008) show that establishments with fewer than 250 workers account for almost three-quarters of the workforce.

(continued)

135

(continued)

Employment by Size of Establishment

Establishment Size by Number	Percent of All Workers Employed
1 to 4	6.9
5 to 9	8.3
10 to 19	11.3
20 to 49	17.4
50 to 99	13.5
100 to 249	16.7
250 to 499	9.3
500 to 999	6.5
1,000 or more	10.2

Another factor to keep in mind is that job turnover tends to be faster in small establishments and small businesses, so they create more job *openings*. Economists have shown that young businesses, which usually are still small, create the most jobs. Don't make the mistake of thinking only in terms of large, established employers.

Skills Required in Major Industries

The following table lists 28 skills from the Department of Labor's O*NET database. Although not all of these skills use the exact same names as the skills you reviewed in Chapter 2, they are similar.

Find the adaptive and transferable skills you listed as your strongest in Chapter 2. Then find the equivalent skills in the following table. (Each skill is listed with a brief definition.) Finally, note the names of the industries for which your top skills are important. If an industry turns up more than once, it is probably a good match for your skills.

Skill	Definition	Industries for Which Skill Is Important
Active Listening	Listening to what other people are saying and asking questions as appropriate.	Banking; Health Care; Social Assistance, Except Child Day Care

Skill	Definition	Industries for Which Skill Is Important
Critical Thinking	Using logic and analysis to identify the strengths and weaknesses of different approaches.	Air Transportation
Equipment Maintenance	Performing routine maintenance and determining when and what kind of maintenance is needed.	Food Manufacturing; Mining; Truck Transportation and Warehousing; Agriculture, Forestry, and Fishing; Automobile Dealers; Food Services and Drinking Places; Steel Manufacturing; Construction; Printing; Textile, Textile Product, and Apparel Manufacturing; Chemical Manufacturing, Except Drugs; Motor Vehicle and Parts Manufacturing; Employment Services; Hotels and Other Accommodations
Installation	Installing equipment, machines, wiring, or programs to meet specifications.	Aerospace Product and Parts Manufacturing; Construction; Machinery Manufacturing; Motor Vehicle and Parts Manufacturing; Utilities; Automobile Dealers; Mining; Telecommunications
Instructing	Teaching others how to do something.	Educational Services; Arts, Entertainment, and Recreation
Judgment and Decision Making	Weighing the relative costs and benefits of a potential action.	Securities, Commodities, and Other Investments
Learning Strategies	Using multiple approaches when learning or teaching new things.	Educational Services; Child Day Care Services; Grocery Stores

(continued)

(continued)

Skill	Definition	Industries for Which Skill Is Important
Management of Financial Resources	Determining how money will be spent to get the work done and accounting for these expenditures.	Advertising and Public Relations Services; Management, Scientific, and Technical Consulting Services; Securities, Commodities, and Other Investments; Advocacy, Grantmaking, and Civic Organizations; Wholesale Trade; Grocery Stores; Motion Picture and Video Industries; Broadcasting
Management of Personnel Resources	Motivating, developing, and directing people as they work; identifying the best people for the job.	Grocery Stores; Motion Picture and Video Industries; Clothing, Accessory, and General Merchandise Stores; Broadcasting; Hotels and Other Accommodations; Construction
Mathematics	Using mathematics to solve problems.	Banking; Clothing, Accessory, and General Merchandise Stores; Construction; Wholesale Trade
Negotiation	Bringing others together and trying to reconcile differences.	Wholesale Trade; Advertising and Public Relations Services; Child Day Care Services; Publishing, Except Software; Advocacy, Grantmaking, and Civic Organizations; Insurance; Arts, Entertainment, and Recreation; Educational Services
Operation and Control	Controlling operations of equipment or systems.	Air Transportation; Printing; Chemical Manufacturing, Except Drugs; Employment Services; Textile, Textile Product, and Apparel Manufacturing; Food Manufacturing; Steel

Skill	Definition	Industries for Which Skill Is Important
		Manufacturing; Agriculture, Forestry, and Fishing; Machinery Manufacturing; Mining; Truck Transportation and Warehousing
Operation Monitoring	Watching gauges, dials, or other indicators to make sure a machine is working properly.	Chemical Manufacturing, Except Drugs; Steel Manufacturing; Textile, Textile Product, and Apparel Manufacturing; Air Transportation; Food Manufacturing; Mining; Motor Vehicle and Parts Manufacturing; Pharmaceutical and Medicine Manufacturing; Printing; Utilities; Aerospace Product and Parts Manufacturing; Agriculture, Forestry, and Fishing; Machinery Manufacturing; Truck Transportation and Warehousing
Persuasion	Persuading others to approach things differently.	Insurance; Securities, Commodities, and Other Investments; Advertising and Public Relations Services; Social Assistance, Except Child Day Care; Educational Services; Publishing, Except Software; Wholesale Trade; Advocacy, Grantmaking, and Civic Organizations; Child Day Care Services
Programming	Writing computer programs for various purposes.	Computer and Electronic Product Manufacturing; Computer Systems Design and Related Services; Employment

(continued)

(continued)

Skill	Definition	Industries for Which Skill Is Important
		Services; Scientific Research and Development Services; Software Publishers; Telecommunications; Hotels and Other Accommodations; Management, Scientific, and Technical Consulting Services; Motion Picture and Video Industries; Food Services and Drinking Places; Automobile Dealers; Grocery Stores
Quality Control Analysis	Evaluating the quality or performance of products, services, or processes.	Machinery Manufacturing; Motor Vehicle and Parts Manufacturing; Pharmaceutical and Medicine Manufacturing; Aerospace Product and Parts Manufacturing; Computer and Electronic Product Manufacturing; Chemical Manufacturing, Except Drugs; Employment Services; Food Manufacturing; Printing; Textile, Textile Product, and Apparel Manufacturing; Steel Manufacturing
Reading Comprehension	Understanding written sentences and paragraphs in work-related documents.	Publishing, Except Software; Air Transportation; Insurance
Repairing	Repairing machines or systems, using the needed tools.	Agriculture, Forestry, and Fishing; Automobile Dealers; Utilities; Construction; Truck Transportation and Warehousing; Mining; Steel Manufacturing; Food Manufacturing;

Skill	Definition	Industries for Which Skill Is Important
		Machinery Manufacturing; Motor Vehicle and Parts Manufacturing; Printing; Textile, Textile Product, and Apparel Manufacturing
Science	Using scientific methods to solve problems.	Pharmaceutical and Medicine Manufacturing; Scientific Research and Development Services
Service Orientation	Actively looking for ways to help people.	Banking; Food Services and Drinking Places; Health Care; Hotels and Other Accommodations; Insurance; Arts, Entertainment, and Recreation; Social Assistance, Except Child Day Care; Advocacy, Grantmaking, and Civic Organizations; Air Transportation; Securities, Commodities, and Other Investments; Wholesale Trade; Employment Services
Social Perceptiveness	Being aware of others' reactions and under-standing why they react the way they do.	Advocacy, Grantmaking, and Civic Organizations; Arts, Entertainment, and Recreation; Child Day Care Services; Clothing, Accessory, and General Merchandise Stores; Educational Services; Social Assistance, Except Child Day Care; Grocery Stores; Health Care; Motion Picture and Video Industries; Food Services and Drinking Places; Hotels and Other Accommodations; Banking

(continued)

(continued)

Skill	Definition	Industries for Which Skill Is Important
Speaking	Talking to others to effectively convey information.	Broadcasting; Arts, Entertainment, and Recreation; Banking; Clothing, Accessory, and General Merchandise Stores; Health Care; Motion Picture and Video Industries; Securities, Commodities, and Other Investments
Systems Analysis	Determining how a system should work and how changes will affect outcomes.	Computer Systems Design and Related Services; Scientific Research and Development Services; Software Publishers; Computer and Electronic Product Manufacturing; Telecommunications; Management, Scientific, and Technical Consulting Services; Aerospace Product and Parts Manufacturing; Utilities
Systems Evaluation	Looking at many indicators of system performance and taking into account their accuracy.	Management, Scientific, and Technical Consulting Services; Computer Systems Design and Related Services; Scientific Research and Development Services; Software Publishers; Computer and Electronic Product Manufacturing; Food Services and Drinking Places; Pharmaceutical and Medicine Manufacturing; Telecommunications
Technology Design	Generating or adapting equipment and technology to serve user needs.	Software Publishers; Computer Systems Design and Related Services

Skill	Definition	Industries for Which Skill Is Important
Time Management	Managing one's own time and the time of others.	Broadcasting; Advertising and Public Relations Services; Publishing, Except Software
Troubleshooting	Determining what is causing an operating error and deciding what to do about it.	Telecommunications; Automobile Dealers; Aerospace Product and Parts Manufacturing; Computer Systems Design and Related Services; Pharmaceutical and Medicine Manufacturing; Truck Transportation and Warehousing; Utilities; Agriculture, Forestry, and Fishing; Chemical Manufacturing, Except Drugs; Computer and Electronic Product Manufacturing; Software Publishers
Writing	Communicating effectively with others in writing as indicated by the needs of the audience.	Broadcasting; Publishing, Except Software; Clothing, Accessory, and General Merchandise Stores; Insurance; Advertising and Public Relations Services; Child Day Care Services; Health Care; Social Assistance, Except Child Day Care; Management, Scientific, and Technical Consulting Services; Scientific Research and Development Services

Review 43 Major Industries

This section contains a list of 43 major industries that cover most of the labor market. Complete the checklist that follows to get some ideas about what industries you should consider more closely.

CHECKLIST OF INDUSTRIES TO CONSIDER IN MORE DETAIL

The first column lists the industry. The next three columns allow you to decide how interested you are in working in that industry or in learning more about it. If an industry does not interest you at all, put a check mark in the "No Interest" column. If that industry interests you somewhat or you are not sure, put a check mark in the "Somewhat Interested" column. If that industry seems very interesting to you, put a check mark in the "Very Interested" column.

Industry to Consider	No Interest	Somewhat Interested	Very Interested
GOODS-PRODUCING INDUSTRIES			
Natural Resources, Construction, and Utilities			
Agriculture, Forestry, and Fishing			
Construction			
Mining			
Utilities			
Manufacturing			
Aerospace Product and Parts Manufacturing			
Chemical Manufacturing, Except Drugs			
Computer and Electronic Product Manufacturing			
Food Manufacturing			
Machinery Manufacturing			
Motor Vehicle and Parts Manufacturing			
Pharmaceutical and Medicine Manufacturing			
Printing			
Steel Manufacturing			
Textile, Textile Product, and Apparel Manufacturing			
SERVICE-PRODUCING INDUSTRIES			
Trade			
Automobile Dealers			
Clothing, Accessory, and General Merchandise Stores			

Industry to Consider	No Interest	Somewhat Interested	Very Interested
Grocery Stores			
Wholesale Trade			
Transportation and Warehousing			
Air Transportation			
Truck Transportation and Warehousing			
Information			
Broadcasting			
Motion Picture and Video Industries			
Publishing, Except Software			
Software Publishers			
Telecommunications			
Financial Activities			
Banking			
Insurance			
Securities, Commodities, and Other Investments			
Professional and Business Services			
Advertising and Public Relations Services			
Computer Systems Design and Related Services			
Employment Services			
Management, Scientific, and Technical Consulting Services			
Scientific Research and Development Services			
Education, Health, and Social Services			
Child Day Care Services			
Educational Services			
Health Care			
Social Assistance, Except Child Day Care			
Leisure and Hospitality			
Arts, Entertainment, and Recreation			
Food Services and Drinking Places			
Hotels and Other Accommodations			

(continued)

(continued)

Industry to Consider	No Interest	Somewhat Interested	Very Interested
Government and Advocacy, Grantmaking, and Civic Organizations			
Advocacy, Grantmaking, and Civic Organizations			
Federal Government			
State and Local Government, Except Education and Health			

Write in any other industries that interest you that are not in this checklist:

_____

Now identify the industries you most want to learn about. Review the checklist and select the five industries that you most want to consider in your ideal career and write them here.

1. _____

   _____

2. _____

   _____

3. _____

   _____

4. _____

   _____

5. _____

   _____

Learn More About Targeted Industries

Details on the industries in the checklist you completed are tracked by the U.S. Department of Labor. Helpful descriptions for these industries appear in an online government publication titled *Career Guide to Industries,* which is updated every two years. You can find it at www.bls.gov/oco/cg.

The industry descriptions in these resources include the following information:

- Significant points
- Nature of the industry
- Working conditions
- Employment
- Occupations in the industry
- Training and advancement
- Outlook
- Earnings
- Sources of additional information

If you decide to do more industry research later, here are some steps you can take to get the most out of the descriptions in the *Career Guide to Industries:*

- **Print them out and mark them up.** Circle or underline anything that is particularly important to you, such as the pay rates, skills, education, or training required.

- **Include important requirements in your interviews and resume.** Later, when you are looking for a job in this industry, emphasize the points you underlined that are also important to employers. For example, do you have the skills that this industry requires? Do you have related interests, experience, or education? Can you mention important trends to indicate your knowledge of the industry?

- **Pay particular attention to the related jobs.** While some jobs are found in most industries (such as accountants, administrative support, and clerical workers), industry-related jobs are listed under the Employment heading.

- **Consider pay, growth, and other factors.** I mentioned earlier that some industries pay better than others. So consider working in an industry that pays better than average, particularly if you find it of interest. You should also, of course, consider other factors, such as industry growth and stability. For example, government jobs tend to be more stable than jobs in industries that are more sensitive to changes in the economy.

Key Points: Chapter 7

- The industry you work in is often as important as the job you choose because of pay, stability, your skills, your interest in it, and other factors.

- More than 80 percent of all employment is in the service-providing sector, and this is where much of the future growth is projected to occur.

- Smaller employers—those with fewer than 250 workers—employ almost 75 percent of the workforce.

- You may be more successful in industries that match your adaptive and transferable skills.

- Use the *Career Guide to Industries* to learn more about the industries that interest you most.

Chapter 8

Overnight Career Choice Matrix and Action Plan

In previous chapters, you've considered various factors that can define what you want in your ideal job. In this chapter, you'll put them all together so that you can find your career focus.

Keep in mind, however, that career planning is an imperfect process that may require you to ultimately compromise and take some chances. Although being completely satisfied with anything is not part of the human condition, this chapter pulls together a combination of things to increase the possibility of selecting a job that fits you well.

You've already seen the suggestion that you should combine a job with the type of organization or industry in which you have an interest. For example, if you have experience or training in accounting and love airplanes, you might consider looking for an accounting-related position in the aircraft manufacturing industry, an agency monitoring airline safety, or in an industry that provides materials or services to the aircraft industry. There are many other possibilities you may think of if you combine those three elements: job, industry/organization type, and interest.

You can do the same thing with the ideal job factors you identified earlier in this book. For example, if you have experience in marketing and love to cook in your free time, it may make sense for you to look for a position in a food or restaurant-related industry. Combining a type of job with an industry that interests you can make a lot of sense.

In a similar way, you can also combine a type of job with several or all of the factors important in an ideal job. You considered these factors in Chapters 2 through 5, and they include

1. Skills and abilities

2. Interests

3. Personal values

4. Preferred earnings

5. Level of responsibility

6. Location

7. Special knowledge

8. Work environment

9. Types of people you like to work with or for

Summarize the Characteristics of Your Ideal Career

This section helps you gather your thoughts and narrow down your ideal career. Answer each question by including those things you identified as being most important to you in the activities you worked through earlier in this book. In some cases, such as the question about skills, you may need to review previous chapters to refresh your memory.

Use this worksheet to clarify the characteristics of a career choice that is a good match for you in several ways. Answer each question by including only those two or three things that are most important to you.

MY IDEAL CAREER

1. What skills or abilities do you most want to use or include in your career? Refer to Chapter 2 if needed.

   Adaptive skills or abilities:

   _____

   _____

   _____

   Transferable skills or abilities:

   _____

   _____

   _____

Job-related skills or abilities:

_____

_____

_____

2. What sorts of things interest you that you may want to include or pursue in your ideal career? Refer to Chapter 3 if needed.

_____

_____

_____

3. What values are particularly important for you to include or pursue in your ideal career? Refer to Chapter 4 if needed.

_____

_____

_____

4. What range of earnings do you expect or prefer? Refer to Chapter 5 if needed.

_____

5. What level of responsibility would you prefer in your work? Refer to Chapter 5 if needed.

_____

_____

6. What location or geographic characteristics would you prefer? Refer to Chapter 5 if needed.

_____

_____

(continued)

(continued)

7. What special knowledge or interests would you like to use or pursue in your ideal career? Refer to Chapter 5 if needed.

   _____

   _____

8. What type of work environment do you prefer? Refer to Chapter 5 if needed.

   _____

   _____

9. What types of people would you prefer to work with or for? Refer to Chapter 5 if needed.

   _____

   _____

THE THREE MOST IMPORTANT THINGS TO INCLUDE IN MY IDEAL CAREER

After you have completed the preceding worksheet, select the three and only three things that are *most* important to include in your ideal career. Write those three things here:

1. _____

2. _____

3. _____

Put Your Ideal Career Characteristics into Graphic Form with the Career Wheel

This optional activity takes the factors you listed in the previous section and puts them into graphic form. For some people, a graphic form can help them better remember and use the information. Fill in the career wheel with your responses.

My ideal job would include the following:

The Career Wheel

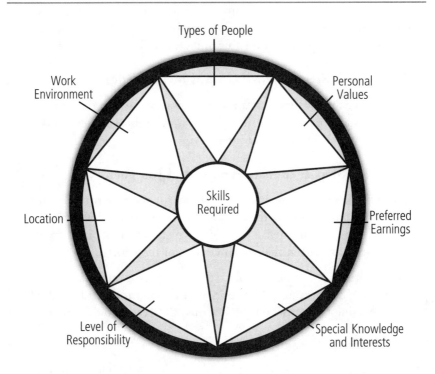

Brainstorm Combinations with the Overnight Career Choice Matrix

The Overnight Career Choice Matrix that follows will help you brainstorm creative combinations of job title, industry, and the ideal job factors you identified earlier.

Tip: *Be creative with the Overnight Career Choice Matrix. Don't be afraid to brainstorm and take some chances—it's all just on paper at this point.*

OVERNIGHT CAREER CHOICE MATRIX

The Overnight Career Choice Matrix has three columns and six rows. You can make your own matrix on separate sheets of paper and include more rows and columns that combine more factors. Use the matrix to come up with interesting and creative job possibilities.

Step 1: Work Groups or Job Titles

Chapter 6 helped you select career interest areas and job titles that interest you. In the top row of the matrix, write three specific work group names or job titles that interest you the most.

Step 2: Industries and Ideal Job Factors

Down the left side of the matrix are spaces for you to write. The first three rows provide spaces for you to write the names of industries from Chapter 7 that interest you. Write the name of one industry in each space provided in the first three rows of the matrix.

Next, write three factors you selected as being most important to include in your next job. Write one most important factor in each of the remaining three rows on the Overnight Career Choice Matrix.

Step 3: Be Creative

Now it is time to get creative. Let's say you wrote "Public Relations Specialist" as a job title and "Agriculture" as a top industry (because you grew up on a farm and know a lot about this). The box in the upper-left corner is where these two items intersect. In that box, write any possible jobs that might combine the job of Public Relations Specialist in the Agriculture industry. Can you think of anything? A few obvious combinations might occur to you, like "PR for an agricultural chemical company" or "PR for a government ag program," as well as some that may not be so obvious. Write anything that occurs to you in that box, even if it seems unrealistic or silly.

Then go to the next box, either down or across (whatever makes more sense to you), and repeat the process for a new combination of factors to consider. For example, let's say you wrote "cross-country bicycle racing" in the fourth row down because that is something you love to do in your free time. Can you think of any jobs that would combine

Public Relations Specialist with bicycle racing? Here are some: "PR for a bicycle manufacturer or parts supplier" and "promoting races" and "building interest in cycling by working for a bicycle racing association."

Repeat this same process for each and every box on your Overnight Career Choice Matrix, writing any job ideas that combine the two elements that intersect in each box.

Overnight Career Choice Matrix

	Work Group or Job Title	Work Group or Job Title	Work Group or Job Title
Top Industry			
Top Industry			
Top Industry			
Ideal Job Factor			
Ideal Job Factor			
Ideal Job Factor			

(continued)

(continued)

Step 4: Identify the Combinations That Make the Most Sense to You

Some job combinations won't make much sense or will not seem interesting or practical to you. This is your matrix, so ignore those and circle the ones that make sense to you as possible ideal careers. Remember that you can use additional sheets of paper if needed.

Some of the combinations may seem unreasonably difficult to achieve or to find. But, if a combination interests you, you might be surprised at how well you might be received by an employer who needs someone with that odd combination of interests. For example, if you were to enter "amateur bicycle racing association" in the search box of your Web browser, you would find several interesting Web sites of organizations and businesses that are very much involved in this sort of activity. Among them is www.usacycling.org, a site that links to bicycle-racing clubs around the world, bicycle racing parts suppliers, and other related sites.

Find the right people in these settings, and many of them will be happy to help you. Some will give you job leads, some will teach you about what they do and where someone like you might fit in the field, many will accept e-mail and a resume from you, and a few will be willing to interview you.

If you want a career having to do with bicycle racing in some way (or in a variety of other improbable combinations of things that interest you), there are real opportunities. And, if you think about it, if you were an employer in the bicycle racing industry who needed someone with public relations, accounting, warehousing, or sales experience, wouldn't you rather hire someone who loves bicycle racing? Yes, you would, and that will be your competitive edge if you seek the right career for the right reasons.

Your Ideal Job Definition

In the spaces that follow, write your definition of your ideal job. Refer to the information you summarized in this chapter as needed.

My ideal career is as a _____ in the
(job title)

_____industry,
(industry)

using my _____skills and background.
(key skills and special knowledge)

My _____ interests and
(key interests)

_____ skills make me well-
(other skills)

qualified for this career. As part of this career, I would like to

_____. I would
(key values)

enjoy a _____ work
(preferred work environment)

environment in _____. I
(preferred geographic location/area)

would like to have _____
(level of responsibility)

responsibility and work with _____
(types of co-workers)

people. I would like to earn at least _____.
(salary)

The activities you just completed help you clearly define the preferred characteristics of your ideal career. Pursuing a career that is in major conflict with one or more of these factors can lead to job failure or unhappiness. So be clear about what you would prefer in your career focus, even if it changes in the future.

Your Overnight Career Choice Action Plan

Now that you have assembled the components of your ideal career, your task is to decide the next step.

Find Your Ideal Job

For many people, the next step is finding a job that comes as close as possible to meeting their ideal career criteria. If you conduct a creative job search, you won't be looking for a job but for *the right* job. Of course, you may need to make some compromise between the ideal and what you accept. But the closer you can come to finding a job that meets your preferences, the better that job will be for you.

> **Tip:** *Part of the search for your ideal job is using a clear job objective on your resumes and applications. The next chapter helps you with that task.*

After completing this book, you may realize that your current job can become your ideal job—or at least more acceptable—with a few changes. For example, would a promotion or a transfer make your current position more ideal for you? If you took on added responsibility, would your job become more interesting to you? Consider these and similar points when deciding your next move.

Pursue More Education or Training

Maybe your ideal job requires more education or training than you have. While it may seem like a huge or even impossible task to go back to school, break this goal into steps or consider it from another point of view.

Suppose, for example, that you want to be a recreational therapist, which combines your skill in art with your interest in social services and health. Within 60 days, your goal might be to find a source of schooling to prepare you for the occupation and to learn about loans and financing options. That might involve some library or Internet research as well as visits to schools. A one-year goal may be to be enrolled in a school, and a two-year goal may be to continue schooling full time and get a part-time job related to your interest to pay the bills. Keep at it and in a few years you will be a recreational therapist.

Or, perhaps, you would like to be a librarian but are not interested in or able to pursue a master's degree. After researching related jobs, you may decide to become a library technician instead.

The Cost of Education and Training

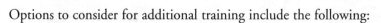

Don't be discouraged if you can't afford the expense of more education. Remember that there are many sources of financial aid, scholarships, loans, and grants. One place to start your research is www.studentaid. ed.gov.

Options to consider for additional training include the following:

- Learn a trade or job while you work, through on-the-job training and work experience.

- Enroll in an apprenticeship or other program that combines on-the-job training with classroom instruction.

- Attend a vocational or technical school to learn job skills such as medical technology, computer repair, auto mechanics, or office skills.

- Participate in accredited online learning programs, accelerated programs, or night classes. Investigate local programs in your area, ask people you know for program recommendations, and consult your librarian for good information sources for more research.

- Get training and work experience in the armed forces.

- Pursue related volunteer work, internships, informal self-study, and earlier leisure activities to develop job skills.

Take Interim Steps

What if you can't change jobs right now? Perhaps, for example, family or other commitments prevent you from pursuing your ideal career. As noted earlier, start taking small steps toward your chosen career.

Perhaps you can job-shadow someone in the field, do informational interviews to learn more about related careers, do related volunteer or part-time work, and join relevant professional associations. Subscribe to industry publications, read books and Internet sites about the career and the field, and attend related trade shows and other events. These experiences will give you valuable experience, knowledge, and contacts for your future career.

Write down some tasks and put timelines on them. For example, research education options over the next 30 days. Or spend four hours a week contacting people in the industries identified in your matrix and asking them for interviews. Write down what you could accomplish in three months, six months, one year, and two years. The important thing is to set a goal and get started.

Deciding to do something next—even if it is not your ideal job—is better than doing nothing.

Do More Career Research

You may decide that you need more information about your ideal career, whether on the skills required, the training needed, or other factors. Many resources, including books, videos, professional associations, other people, and online information, can help you. See Appendix B for recommended career information resources.

Key Points: Chapter 8

- Career planning is an imperfect process that may require you to ultimately compromise and take some chances.

- You might be surprised at how well your combination of interests, skills, values, and other characteristics will be received by an employer.

- After you formulate your ideal career definition, your next steps may include finding a job that matches it, pursuing more education or training, or taking interim steps to achieve your goal.

- Plan to do something specific, soon, to move you toward your goal.

Chapter 9

Write Your Job Objective

Although most of this book is about exploring career options, this chapter is more about preparing for the job search. You can find many excellent books about job-hunting techniques (JIST Publishing specializes in this topic), but the goal of this chapter is to help you translate what you've done so far into terms that will be useful during your job search. You'll learn how to clearly communicate your career choice in a format most employers will value.

For example, your resume needs to clearly answer the employer's question, "Who are you and what can you do for me?" It's difficult to write a job objective that does not exclude you from jobs you would consider yet does not sound as if you are willing to do just about anything. Including a clear, focused job objective is quite helpful to people reading your resume.

Avoid a Self-Centered, "Gimme" Approach

Many poorly conceived job objectives emphasize what the person wants but don't provide information on what the person *can do*. For example, an objective that says "Interested in a position that allows me to be creative and offers adequate pay and advancement opportunities" is not a good objective at all. Who cares? This objective (a real one that someone actually wrote) displays a self-centered, "gimme" approach that turns off most employers.

> **Note:** *While the language about what you want in a job is part of your ideal career definition, it's not something to share completely with employers. When you look for a job, start researching organizations, and begin interviewing, you can use the information you learn about an employer to see whether the job fits your other ideal-career criteria.*

Sample Job Objectives

Look through the following examples of simple but useful job objectives. Most provide some information on the type of job the person is seeking, as well as the skills he or she offers. The best ones avoid a narrow job title and keep options open to a wide variety of possibilities within a range of appropriate jobs.

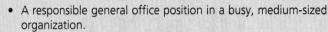

Sample Job Objectives

- A responsible general office position in a busy, medium-sized organization.

- A management position in the warehousing industry. Position should require supervisory, problem-solving, and organizational skills.

- Computer programming and/or systems analysis. Prefer an accounting-oriented emphasis and a solutions-oriented organization.

- Medical assistant or secretary in a physician's office, hospital, or other health services environment.

- Responsible position requiring skills in public relations, writing, and reporting.

- An aggressive and success-oriented professional seeking a sales position offering both challenge and growth.

- Desire position in the office management, administrative support, or clerical area. Position should require flexibility, good organizational skills, and an ability to handle people.

If you are custom-writing your resume for a specific position, you can cleverly say something like "To obtain a position as [insert position title being sought here] with [insert employer name here]."

Five Tips for Writing a Good Job Objective

The job objective you write should fit your career focus. But here are some general things to consider when you write it.

1. **Avoid job titles.** Job titles such as "receptionist" or "marketing analyst" can involve very different activities in different organizations. If your resume says your objective is to be a receptionist, you will probably not be considered for such jobs as "office manager" or "marketing assistant," even though you could do them. It is best to use broad categories of jobs rather than specific titles so that you can be considered for a wide variety of positions related to the skills you have. For example, instead of "receptionist," you could say "responsible

office-management or clerical position," if that's what you would really consider and are qualified for.

2. **Define a "bracket of responsibility" to include the potential for upward mobility.** Although you might be willing to accept a variety of jobs related to your skills, you should definitely include jobs that require higher levels of responsibility and pay. The earlier example would allow the candidate to be considered for an office-management position as well as for office-support and clerical jobs. In effect, you should define a "bracket of responsibility" in your objective that includes the range of jobs you are willing to accept. This bracket should include the lower range of jobs you would consider, as well as those that require higher levels of responsibility, up to and including the most responsible job you think you could handle. Even if you have not been given those higher levels of responsibility in the past, many employers will consider you for them if you have the skills to handle them.

3. **Include your most important skills.** What are the most important skills needed for the job you want? Include one or more of these in your job objective statement. The implication is that if you are looking for a job that *requires* "organizational skills," then you must have those skills. Of course, your interview (and resume or job application) should give evidence that you have those skills through specific examples.

4. **Include specifics only if they really matter to you.** If you have substantial experience in a particular industry (such as "computer-controlled machine tools") or you have a narrow, specific objective that you *really* want (such as "art therapist with the mentally handicapped"), it's okay to say so. If that's what you want, it's worth pursuing. But you should realize that narrowing your alternatives might keep you from being considered for other jobs for which you

> **Tip:** If you are writing a chronological resume, you may want to include a "summary," "profile," or other introductory section instead of an objective. A chronological resume lists your work experience in reverse order, starting with the most recent experience.
>
> If you're writing a skills/functional resume, a job objective statement becomes more important because the job you want is less obvious on your resume. A skills/functional resume organizes your experience by types of skills and is better to use if your work experience has gaps or is diverse.

qualify. It would still be a good idea to have a second, more general objective ready, just in case.

5. **Be clear about the job you want.** While this book has helped you find your career focus, I encourage you to read more-detailed descriptions of your target career. The descriptions will contain skills to emphasize on your resume and in interviews. The *Occupational Outlook Handbook,* created by the U.S. Department of Labor, contains full narratives on the 288 jobs briefly described in Chapter 6. It's a very good source of information, and you can find it in library reference sections and bookstores, as well as on the Department of Labor's Web site at www.bls.gov/oco/home.htm. JIST sells a reasonably priced reprint of the *OOH* (with some additional content) at www.jist.com or 1-800-648-JIST.

Construct Your Job Objective

Use the following worksheet to help you construct an effective and accurate job objective statement for your resume.

My Job Objective

Complete each of the following items. When you're done, you'll have a better idea of what to include in your resume's job objective statement.

1. **What sort of position, title, and area of specialization do you want?** Write the type of job you want, just as you might explain it to someone you know.

   _____

   _____

   _____

2. **Define your bracket of responsibility.** Describe the range of jobs you would accept, from the minimum up to those you think you could handle if you were given the chance.

_____

_____

_____

3. **Name the key skills you have that are important in this job.** Identify the two or three key skills that are particularly important for success in the job that you are seeking. Select one or more of these that you are strong in and that you enjoy using. Write it (or them) here.

_____

_____

_____

4. **Name specific areas of expertise or strong interests that you want to use in your next job.** If you have substantial interest, experience, or training in a specific area and want to include it in your job objective (remembering that it might limit your options), write it here.

_____

_____

_____

5. **What else is important to you?** Is there anything else you want to include in your job objective? This could be a value that is particularly important to you such as "a position that allows me to help families," "employment in an aggressive and results-oriented organization," or "a small- to mid-size business."

_____

_____

_____

Finalize Your Job Objective

Most employers are impressed by candidates who are very clear about the jobs they want and why they want them. A good job objective may help to keep your resume out of the trash bin. Few interviews end well unless the interviewer is convinced that you really want the job and have the skills to do it. For that reason, it is essential to have a clear job objective.

Tip: *Although a simple chronological resume does not require a career objective, a skills resume does. Without a reasonably clear job objective, you cannot select and organize the key skills you have to support that objective.*

Using your answers from the preceding worksheet, write your job objective here. You can fine-tune it later if needed.

Job objective: _____

_____

_____

_____

_____

_____

Now that you have clarified your career focus and your job objective, you can go out and get interviews for jobs that closely approximate what you want. In interviews, support your interest in the job by presenting the skills and experiences you have and the advantages you present over other candidates. It sounds simple enough—and it can be—as long as you are clear about what job you want to do and are well organized about finding it.

A Few Final Comments

You really can complete all of this book in one day and have a clearer career objective overnight.

But career management is never really complete, because we change over time and unexpected opportunities arise. We gain more experience, learn more about what we do and do not want, shed or gain responsibilities, get bored and develop new interests, make new contacts, and hear about new possibilities we haven't previously considered. So whatever makes sense for you today may change over time. Our lives interact with our careers; it is simply the way things are.

So do "sleep" overnight on whatever you have learned about career planning from this book today. Understand that it is not important to know precisely what you want to do forever. Instead, think about what is important to you now and ask yourself, "What do I want to do next?" as a way of setting your course for the future.

Key Points: Chapter 9

- Write a job objective from an employer's point of view: What sorts of things can you do, and what skills, experience, and other assets do you offer? Writing a brief and well-done job objective for your resume will help you later in interviews and the job search.

- Be careful to not write a job objective with a self-centered, "gimme" approach, which turns off most employers.

- Five tips for writing your job objective include avoiding job titles, defining a "bracket of responsibility," including your most important skills, including specifics only if they really matter to you, and being clear about the job you want.

Job Exploration Worksheet

This worksheet helps you collect additional information on specific jobs. Make one photocopy of the worksheet for each job title you research. Start by getting more information on the jobs you listed in "My Top Job Titles" in Chapter 6. Use the reference sources listed elsewhere in this book or in Appendix B.

JOB EXPLORATION WORKSHEET

Basic Information on This Job

Job title _____

Interest area _____

Source(s) of information used to research this job _____

_____

More Information on This Job

What do people in this job do? _____

_____

_____

_____

_____

_____

(continued)

(continued)

Key skills and abilities this job requires _____

_____

_____

Training, education, other qualifications needed _____

_____

Projected growth rate_____

Average earnings (national) _____

Working conditions_____

_____

Level of responsibility _____

_____

Does this job incorporate your top interests?_____

_____

Is this job likely to take advantage of your special knowledge?_____

_____

Is this job likely to include your most important values? _____

_____

Types of co-workers that you will most likely have at this job_____

_____

Is this job most likely available in a location you desire? _____

_____

Related jobs _____

_____

Your Observations

What are the negatives about this job for you? _____

_____

What are the positives about this job for you? _____

_____

On a scale of 1 to 10, how interested are you in this job in relation to others? _____

What more do need to know about this job before you can make a decision? _____

_____

_____

_____

What barriers would you face in getting this job, and how might you overcome them? _____

_____

_____

_____

Would you be able to get this job now? If not, what jobs or other experience could you get to help you prepare for this job? _____

_____

_____

What could you do *now* to begin preparing for this job? _____

_____

_____

_____

Sources of More Career Information

This book has helped you define your career focus. Still, you may want to learn more about your career choice, explore related career options, or be well-prepared for a future career change. Career research helps you accomplish these goals and more. By doing more career research, you also

- **Increase opportunities in your job search by identifying a wider range of job targets.** With thousands of specialized job titles, you are almost certain to overlook a number of them that would fit your needs very well. Looking up a few job titles is a start, but reviewing more jobs within clusters of similar jobs is likely to help you identify jobs you don't know much about but that would be good ones for you to consider.

- **Find skills from previous jobs to support your present objective.** Look up descriptions for jobs you have had in the past. A careful reading will help you to identify skills you used that can be transferred and used in the new job. Even "minor" jobs can be helpful in this way. For example, if you waited on tables while going to school, you would discover that doing this job requires the ability to work under pressure, deal with customers, work quickly, have good communication, and many other skills. If, for example, you were now looking for a job as an accountant, you can see how transferable skills used in an apparently unrelated past job (such as waiting on tables) can be used to support your ability to do another job.

- **Improve your interviewing skills.** Sure, you may think you know what's involved in a particular job, but that is not the same as preparing for an interview. Most people with substantial education, training, and work experience in a particular field do not do a good job of presenting their skills in the interview. People who do their homework by carefully reading a job description and then mentioning key skills that the job requires in an interview often get job offers over those with better credentials. Why? Because they do a more convincing job in the interview, and they make it easier for an employer to understand why they should hire this job seeker over another.

- **Find the typical salary range, trends, and other details for jobs.** The descriptions will help you to know what pay range to expect, as well as many other details about the job and trends that are affecting it. But note that your local pay and other details can differ significantly from the national information provided.

- **Write a better resume.** Knowing the specific skills a job requires allows you to focus on those skills in your resume.

The better-prepared job seeker often gets the job over those with better credentials. Remember this, and consider doing more homework on your job options now and throughout your job search.

Major Sources of Job Descriptions and Related Information

While hundreds of sources of career information exist, the books described in this section offer most of what you need. All books are available at most bookstores and libraries or from JIST Publishing at www.jist.com or 800-648-JIST.

Occupational Outlook Handbook

If you use only one reference book, this should be it. Published by the Department of Labor and updated every two years, the *OOH* provides more than 280 longer descriptions of the major jobs listed in Chapter 6. Each job narrative includes information on the skills required; pay rates; projections for growth; education and training required; working conditions; advancement opportunities; related jobs; and job-specific sources of additional information, including Web sites. The *OOH* is available in most schools, libraries, career counseling centers, and bookstores. The *OOH* content is available online at www.bls.gov/oco/home.htm. JIST's reprint of the *OOH* includes a personality assessment and additional material on emerging jobs.

JIST offers targeted career information based on the *OOH* in its "Top Careers" series: *Top 300 Careers* and *100 Fastest-Growing Careers.*

*Occupational Information Network (O*NET)*

This database, maintained by the U.S. Department of Labor, contains specific information on hundreds of data elements for more than 900 job titles. A book called the *O*NET Dictionary of Occupational Titles* (published by JIST) offers the only complete printed source of the O*NET descriptions. Descriptions include details on related skills, earnings, abilities, education, projected growth, and more. You can access the O*NET job descriptions online at http://online.onetcenter.org.

Enhanced Occupational Outlook Handbook

The *EOOH* is a good all-in-one reference that includes the job descriptions from the *OOH*, plus descriptions of related jobs from the Department of Labor's O*NET database (about 800 jobs) and from the U.S. Department of Labor's *Dictionary of Occupational Titles* (about 1,700 descriptions). This resource is ideal for in-depth career research because it includes 8,000 job descriptions—more than in any other book.

Best Jobs for the 21st Century

This best-selling book emphasizes jobs with fast growth, high pay, and large numbers of openings. It includes more than 500 descriptions plus many useful "best jobs" lists, such as highest paying, best overall, and best at various levels of education. Other books in this series include *200 Best Jobs for College Graduates, 300 Best Jobs Without a Four-Year Degree, 50 Best Jobs for Your Personality, 200 Best Jobs Through Apprenticeships,* and *150 Best Jobs Through Military Training.*

Career Guide to Industries

This online-only book by the U.S. Department of Labor reviews trends, jobs, and earnings in the 43 major industries listed in Chapter 7. You can find the industry descriptions at www.bls.gov/oco/cg/home.htm.

Other Helpful Career and Education Books

Other useful books for career and education information include the following titles.

College Majors Handbook with Real Career Paths and Payoffs. This best-selling book by Neeta Fogg, Paul Harrington, and Thomas Harrington is based on an enormous study of 150,000 college graduates. The authors used this information to create a practical guide on the actual jobs and earnings of college graduates in 60 majors. The result is the most accurate facts available on long-term outcomes associated with particular majors.

Guide to America's Federal Jobs. This resource by Bruce Maxwell and the Editors at JIST takes you through the federal job-finding process.

Same-Day Resume, 30-Day Job Promotion, and *Next-Day Job Interview.* These popular guides in JIST's *Help in a Hurry* series help you find a good job quickly.

The Twitter Job Search Guide. Now that "tweets" are the fastest-growing form of communication, it's time for you to learn how to exploit this resource in your job-hunting efforts. This book by Susan Britton Whitcomb is packed with useful suggestions.

Other Research Options

You can find career information at libraries, at school career centers, through professional associations (which are listed in the *OOH*), and from people you know who work in jobs that interest you.

The Internet offers a multitude of career sites. Start with the Department of Labor's site at www.bls.gov, which includes access to the job descriptions in the *OOH* and other labor market information. Then visit the Career OneStop site at www.careeronestop.org, where you can learn about occupations (including local information), educational and training options, and job hunting.

Index

A

Accountants and Auditors, 67, 90
action plan, 157–159
active listening skills, 136
Actors, Producers, and Directors, 81, 84
Actuaries, 95
adaptive skills, 18–21, 25
Administrative Services Managers, 90
Advertising, Marketing, Promotions, Public Relations, and Sales Managers, 118
Advertising Sales Agents, 86
Agricultural and Food Scientists, 76
Agricultural Inspectors, 73
Agricultural Workers, Other, 74
Agriculture and Natural Resources career cluster, 44, 73–76
Air Traffic Controllers, 122
Aircraft and Avionics Equipment Mechanics and Service Technicians, 124
Aircraft Pilots and Flight Engineers, 124–125
American Association of Counseling and Development, 25
Animal Care and Service Workers, 74
Announcers, 81
Appraisers and Assessors of Real Estate, 118
Architects, Except Landscape and Naval, 80
Architecture and Construction career cluster, 44, 76–81
Archivists, Curators, and Museum Technicians, 120
artistic skills, 126
Artists and Related Workers, 81, 84

Arts and Communication career cluster, 44–45, 81–86
Assemblers and Fabricators, 111
associate degree, 12–14. *See also* postsecondary training
Athletes, Coaches, Umpires, and Related Workers, 91
Athletic Trainers, 101
Atmospheric Scientists, 120
Audiologists, 101
Authors, Writers, and Editors, 84
Automotive Body and Related Repairers, 122
Automotive Service Technicians and Mechanics, 124

B

bachelor's degree, 12–13
  Agriculture and Natural Resources career cluster, 76
  Architecture and Construction career cluster, 80–81
  Arts and Communication career cluster, 84–86
  Business and Administration career cluster, 90–91
  Education and Training career cluster, 92–93
  Finance and Insurance career cluster, 95–96
  Government and Public Administration career cluster, 96
  Health Science career cluster, 101–103
  Human Service career cluster, 107
  Information Technology career cluster, 108–109
  Law and Public Safety career cluster, 111

Retail and Wholesale Sales and Service career cluster, 118–119

Scientific Research, Engineering, and Mathematics career cluster, 120–122

Transportation, Distribution, and Logistics career cluster, 125

Barbers, Cosmetologists, and Other Personal Appearance Workers, 105–106

Best Jobs for the 21st Century, 175

Bill and Account Collectors, 94

Billing and Posting Clerks and Machine Operators, 86

Biological Scientists, 120

Boilermakers, 76

Bookbinders and Bindery Workers, 81–82

Bookkeeping, Accounting, and Auditing Clerks, 86

brainstorming, 153–156

Brickmasons, Blockmasons, and Stonemasons, 77

Broadcast and Sound Engineering Technicians and Radio Operators, 82–83

Brokerage Clerks, 86

Budget Analysts, 90

Building Cleaning Workers, 104

Bus Drivers, 123

Business and Administration career cluster, 45, 86–91

C

Camera and Photographic Equipment Repairers, 111–112

Cardiovascular Technologists and Technicians, 98

career choice, 41

career clues, 50–53

career clusters, 44–50

Career Guide to Industries, 146–147, 175

career information sources, 173–176

career management, 14–15

career research, 159, 173–176

career interim steps, 159

career wheel, 152–153

Cargo and Freight Agents, 86

Carpenters, 77

Carpet, Floor, and Tile Installers and Finishers, 77

Cashiers, 116

Cement Masons, Concrete Finishers, Segmental Pavers, and Terrazzo Workers, 77

Chefs, Head Cooks, and Food Preparation and Serving Supervisors, 104

Chemists and Materials Scientists, 120

Child Care Workers, 105

Chiropractors, 101

Claims Adjusters, Appraisers, Examiners, and Investigators, 94–95

Clinical Laboratory Technologists and Technicians, 98, 101–102

Coin, Vending, and Amusement Machine Servicers and Repairers, 77

college education, 9, 11–12

college experiences, 27–29

College Majors Handbook with Real Career Paths and Payoffs, 175

Commercial and Industrial Designers, 85

communication skills, 126

Communications Equipment Operators, 82

Computer and Information Systems Managers, 108

Computer, Automated Teller, and Office Machine Repairers, 114

Computer Control Programmers and Operators, 112

Computer Network, Systems, and Database Administrators, 108–109

Computer Operators, 108

Computer Software Engineers and Computer Programmers, 109

Computer Support Specialists, 108

Computer Systems Analysts, 109

Computer Scientists, 109

Conservation Scientists and Foresters, 76

Construction and Building Inspectors, 77

Construction Equipment Operators, 77–78

Construction Laborers, 78

Construction Managers, 80

Cooks and Food Preparation Workers, 104

Correctional Officers, 109

Cost Estimators, 80

Counselors, 107

Counter and Rental Clerks, 116

Couriers and Messengers, 86–87

Court Reporters, 110

co-workers, 68–69

Credit Authorizers, Checkers, and Clerks, 94

critical thinking skills, 137

Customer Service Representatives, 87

D

Dancers and Choreographers, 82

Data Entry and Information Processing Workers, 87

Demonstrators and Product Promoters, 116

Dental Assistants, 97

Dental Hygienists, 98

Dentists, 102

Department of Labor, 5, 11–12, 25, 135–136

dependability, 18

Desktop Publishers, 87

Diagnostic Medical Sonographers, 98–99

Diesel Service Technicians and Mechanics, 124

Dietitians and Nutritionists, 102

Dispatchers, Except Police, Fire, and Ambulance, 87

doctorate, 12–13. *See also* bachelor's degree

Drafters, 80

Drywall and Ceiling Tile Installers, Tapers, Plasterers, and Stucco Masons, 78

E

earnings, 10–12, 61–62, 131

Economists, 120

education, 9, 11–14, 27–29, 50–51, 65–66, 158–159

Education Administration, 92

Education and Training career cluster, 45, 91–93

Electrical and Electronics Installers and Repairers, 115

Electricians, 78

Electronic Home Entertainment Equipment Installers and Repairers, 83

elementary school experiences, 26

Elevator Installers and Repairers, 112

Eligibility Interviewers, Government Programs, 106

Emergency Medical Technicians and Paramedics, 99

employer-desired skills, 25

employers, size, 135–136

Engineering and Natural Sciences Managers, 120

Engineering Technicians, 119

Engineers, 121

Enhanced Occupational Outlook Handbook, 175

environment at work, 10, 66–68

Environmental Scientists and Specialists, 76

Epidemiologists, 121

equipment maintenance skills, 137

F

Farmers, Ranchers, and Agricultural Managers, 74, 76

Fashion Designers, 83

File Clerks, 87

Finance and Insurance career cluster, 46, 94–96

Financial Analysts, 95

Financial Managers, 95

Fire Fighters, 109

Fire Inspectors and Investigators, 110

Fishers and Fishing Vessel Operators, 74

Fitness Workers, 92

Flight Attendants, 123

Floral Designers, 74

Food and Beverage Serving and Related Workers, 104

Food Processing Occupations, 74

Food Service Managers, 104

Forest and Conservation Workers, 74–75

full-time workers, 11–12

Funeral Directors, 106

G

Gallop Poll job satisfaction poll, 8

Gaming Cage Workers, 116

Gaming Services Occupations, 83

GED, 11–12

Geoscientists and Hydrologists, 121

Glaziers, 78

goods-producing industries, 132, 134, 144

Government and Public Administration career cluster, 46, 96

Graders and Sorters, Agricultural Products, 75

Graphic Designers, 85

Grounds Maintenance Workers, 75

growth, industry, 132–134

Guide to America's Federal Jobs, 176

H

Hazardous Materials Removal Workers, 75

Health Educators, 107

Health Science career cluster, 46, 97–103

Heating, Air Conditioning, and Refrigeration Mechanics and Installers, 80

Heavy Vehicle and Mobile Equipment Service Technicians and Mechanics, 112

Help in a Hurry series, 176

high school experiences, 27

high school graduates, 9, 11–12

Home Appliance Repairers, 78

Home Health Aides and Personal and Home Care Aides, 106

Hospitality, Tourism, and Recreation career cluster, 47, 104–105

Hotel, Motel, and Resort Desk Clerks, 116

Human Resource Assistants, Except Payroll and Timekeeping, 87

Human Resources, Training, and Labor Relations Managers and Specialists, 90

Human Service career cluster, 47, 105–107

I

ideal job
  career management, 14–15
  characteristics, 69, 150–153
  components, 10
  defining, 5, 156–157
  earnings, 11–12
  education, 11–14
  job satisfaction, 7–9, 15
  job security, 12–13
  job title, 6–7
  life planning, 15
  objective, 6–7, 157, 161–165

success, 13

underemployed, 13

Industrial Machinery Mechanics and Millwrights, 112

Industrial Production Managers, 87–88

industries

goods-producing, 132, 134, 144

importance in job search, 131

projected growth, 132–134

required skills, 136–143

service-producing, 133–135, 144–146

researching, 146–147

Information Technology career cluster, 47, 108–109

Inspectors, Testers, Sorters, Samplers, and Weighers, 112

installation skills, 137

Instructional Coordinators, 93

instructing skills, 137

Insulation Workers, 78

Insurance Sales Agents, 95

Insurance Underwriters, 95–96

interests, 10, 43

career clues, 50–53

career clusters, 44–50

Interior Designers, 84

internships, 11

interpersonal skills, 127

Interpreters and Translators, 91

Interviewers, Except Eligibility and Loan, 88

J

Jewelers and Precious Stone and Metal Workers, 115

job descriptions, 125–128

job-related skills, 18, 25–41

job satisfaction, 7–9, 15

job security, 12–13

job titles, 6–7, 71–73

Judges, Magistrates, and Other Judicial Workers, 111

judgment and decision making skills, 137

K–L

knowledge, special, 10, 65–66

Landscape Architects, 81

Law and Public Safety career cluster, 48, 109–111

Lawyers, 111

learning, online, 11

learning strategies skills, 137

leisure activities, 50–51

Librarians, 93

Library Technicians and Library Assistants, 91–92

Licensed Practical and Licensed Vocational Nurses, 99

life planning, 15

Line Installers and Repairers, 79

Loan Interviewers and Clerks, 94

Loan Officers, 94

location, 10, 64–65

Lodging Managers, 104

Logging Workers, 75

Louis Harris and Associates work-importance poll, 8–9

M

Machine Setters, Operators, and Tenders—Metal and Plastic, 112–113

Machinists, 113

Maintenance and Repair Workers, General, 79

Management Analysts, 91

management of financial resources skills, 138

management of personnel resources skills, 138

managerial skills, 127

Manufacturing career cluster, 48–49, 111–115

Market and Survey Researchers, 118

Massage Therapists, 99

master's degree, 12–13. *See also* bachelor's degree

Material Moving Occupations, 113

mathematics skills, 127, 138

Mathematicians, 121

meaning in work, 15

mechanical skills, 127

Medical and Health Services Managers, 102

Medical Assistants, 97

Medical, Dental, and Ophthalmic Laboratory Technicians, 97

Medical Equipment Repairers, 115

Medical Records and Health Information Technicians, 99

Medical Scientists, 121

Medical Transcriptionists, 99

Meeting and Convention Planners, 118

Meter Readers, Utilities, 88

Models, 116

motivation, 55–59

Musical Instrument Repairers and Tuners, 113

Musicians, Singers, and Related Workers, 82, 85

N

negotiation skills, 138

Next-Day Job Interview, 176

News Analysts, Reporters, and Correspondents, 85

night school, 11

Nuclear Medicine Technologists, 99

Nursing and Psychiatric Aides, 97, 99–100

O

objective in resume, 6–7, 161–167

Occupational Health and Safety Specialists, 102

Occupational Health and Safety Technicians, 119

Occupational Information Network (O*NET), 175

Occupational Outlook Handbook, 128, 174–175

Occupational Therapist Assistants and Aides, 97, 100

Occupational Therapists, 102

Office and Administrative Support Supervisors and Managers, 88

Office Clerks, General, 88

on-the-job training

  Agriculture and Natural Resources career cluster, 73–75

  Architecture and Construction career cluster, 76–80

  Arts and Communication career cluster, 81–83

  Business and Administration career cluster, 86–90

  Education and Training career cluster, 91–92

  Finance and Insurance career cluster, 94

  Health Science career cluster, 97–98

  Hospitality, Tourism, and Recreation career cluster, 104–105

  Human Service career cluster, 105–106

  Information Technology career cluster, 108

  Law and Public Safety career cluster, 109–110

  Manufacturing career cluster, 111–114

  Retail and Wholesale Sales and Service career cluster, 116–117

  Transportation, Distribution, and Logistics career cluster, 122–124

online learning, 11

operation and control skills, 138–139

operation monitoring skills, 139

Operations Research Analysts, 121

Opticians, Dispensing, 97

Optometrists, 102

Order Clerks, 88

organizational skills, 18

Overnight Career Choice Matrix, 153–156

P

Painters and Paperhangers, 79

Painting and Coating Workers, Except Construction and Maintenance, 113

Paralegals and Legal Assistants, 111

Payroll and Timekeeping Clerks, 88

Personal Financial Advisors, 96

personal values, 10, 55–59

personality traits, 19–21

persuasion skills, 139

Pest Control Workers, 75

Pharmacists, 102–103

Pharmacy Technicians and Aides, 97

Photographers, 82

Photographic Process Workers and Processing Machine Operators, 82

Physical Therapist Assistants and Aides, 98, 100

Physical Therapists, 103

Physician Assistants, 103

Physicians and Surgeons, 103

Physicists and Astronomers, 121

Plumbers, Pipelayers, Pipefitters, and Steamfitters, 79

Podiatrists, 103

Police and Detectives, 110–111

Police, Fire, and Ambulance Dispatchers, 110

Postal Service Clerks, 89

Postal Service Mail Carriers, 89

Postal Service Mail Sorters, Processors, and Processing Machine Operators, 89

postsecondary training, 27–29

Architecture and Construction career cluster, 80

Arts and Communication career cluster, 83–84

associate degree, 12–14

Business and Administration career cluster, 90

Education and Training career cluster, 92

Finance and Insurance career cluster, 95

Health Science career cluster, 98–101

Hospitality, Tourism, and Recreation career cluster, 105

Human Service career cluster, 106–107

Information Technology career cluster, 108

Law and Public Safety career cluster, 110–111

Manufacturing career cluster, 114–115

Retail and Wholesale Sales and Service career cluster, 118

Scientific Research, Engineering, and Mathematics career cluster, 119–120

Transportation, Distribution, and Logistics career cluster, 124

Power Plant Operators, Distributors, and Dispatchers, 113

Prepress Technicians and Workers, 83–84

Printing Machine Operators, 83

Private Detectives and Investigators, 110

Probation Officers and Correctional Treatment Specialists, 107

Procurement Clerks, 89

Production, Planning, and Expediting Clerks, 123

professional degree, 12–13. *See also* bachelor's degree

programming skills, 139–140

Property, Real Estate, and Community Association Managers, 118

Psychologists, 107

Public Relations Specialists, 85

Purchasing Managers, Buyers, and Purchasing Agents, 117, 119

Q–R

quality control analysis skills, 140

Radiation Therapists, 100

Radio and Telecommunications Equipment Installers and Repairers, 84

Radiologic Technologists and Technicians, 100

Rail Transportation Occupations, 123

reading comprehension skills, 140

Real Estate Brokers and Sales Agents, 117–118

Receptionists and Information Clerks, 89

Recreation Workers, 106

Recreational Therapists, 103

Registered Nurses, 100

repairing skills, 140–141

Research & Forecasts poll on work values by education level, 9

researching industries, 146–147

Reservation and Transportation Ticket Agents and Travel Clerks, 105

Respiratory Therapists, 100

Respiratory Therapy Technicians, 101

responsibility level, 10, 63

Retail and Wholesale Sales and Service career cluster, 49, 116–119

Retail Salespersons, 117

Roofers, 79

S

salary. *See* earnings

Sales Engineers, 119

Sales Representatives, Wholesale and Manufacturing, 117

Sales Worker Supervisors, 117

Same-Day Resume, 176

satisfaction with job, 7–9, 15

science skills, 127, 141

Science Technicians, 119–120, 122

Scientific Research, Engineering, and Mathematics career cluster, 49, 119–122

Secretaries and Administrative Assistants, 89–90

Securities, Commodities, and Financial Services Sales Agents, 96

Security Guards and Gaming Surveillance Officers, 110

Semiconductor Processors, 115

service orientation skills, 141

service-producing industries, 133–136, 144–146

Sheet Metal Workers, 113

Shipping, Receiving, and Traffic Clerks, 123

short-term certificate programs, 11

skills and abilities, 10, 17–41, 126–127, 136–143

    active listening skills, 136

    adaptive skills/personality traits, 18–21, 25

    artistic skills, 126

    career choice impact, 41

    communication skills, 126

    critical thinking skills, 137

    employer preferences, 25

    equipment maintenance skills, 137

    identifying, 18–41

    industry requirements, 136–143

    installation skills, 137

    instructing skills, 137

    interpersonal skills, 127

    job-related skills, 18, 25–41

judgment and decision making skills,
137

learning strategies skills, 137

management of financial resources skills,
138

management of personnel resources skills,
138

managerial skills, 127

mathematics skills, 127, 138

mechanical skills, 127

negotiation skills, 138

operation and control skills, 138–139

operation monitoring skills, 139

persuasion skills, 139

programming skills, 139–140

quality control analysis skills, 140

reading comprehension skills, 140

repairing skills, 140–141

science skills, 127, 141

service orientation skills, 141

social perceptiveness skills, 141

speaking skills, 142

systems analysis skills, 142

systems evaluation skills, 142

technology design skills, 142

time management skills, 143

transferable skills, 18, 21–25

troubleshooting skills, 143

writing skills, 143

Small Engine Mechanics, 123

Social and Human Service Assistants, 98

social perceptiveness skills, 141

Social Scientists, Other, 122

Social Workers, 107

Sociologists and Political Scientists, 122

sources of career information, 173–176
researching industries, 146–147

speaking skills, 142

Speech-Language Pathologists, 103

Stock Clerks and Order Fillers, 117

Stationary Engineers and Boiler
Operators, 114

Statisticians, 122

Structural and Reinforcing Iron and
Metal Workers, 79

success, 10, 13

Surgical Technologists, 101

Surveyors, Cartographers,
Photogrammetrists, and Surveying and
Mapping Technicians, 79–81

systems analysis skills, 142

systems evaluation skills, 142

T

Tax Examiners, Collectors, and Revenue
Agents, 96

Taxi Drivers and Chauffeurs, 123

Teacher Assistants, 91

Teachers—Adult Literacy and Remedial
Education, 93

Teachers—Kindergarten, Elementary,
Middle, and Secondary, 93

Teachers—Postsecondary, 92–93

Teachers—Preschool, Except Special
Education, 92

Teachers—Self-Enrichment Education,
92

Teachers—Special Education, 93

Teachers—Vocational, 93

Technical Writers, 85

technology design skills, 142

Television, Video, and Motion Picture
Camera Operators and editors, 85–86

Tellers, 94

Textile, Apparel, and Furnishings
Occupations, 114

Theatrical and Performance Makeup
Artists, 106–107

30-Day Job Promotions, 176

time management skills, 143

Tool and Die Makers, 114

Top Executives, 91

training. *See* education

transferable skills, 18, 21–25

Transportation, Distribution, and Logistics career cluster, 49–50, 122–125

Travel Agents, 105

troubleshooting skills, 143

Truck Drivers and Drivers/Sales Workers, 124

trustworthiness, 18

The Twitter Job Search Guide, 176

U–V

underemployed, 13

Urban and Regional Planners, 96

U.S. Department of Labor, 5, 11–12, 25, 175

values, personal, 10, 55–59

Veterinarians, 103

Veterinary Technologists and Technicians, 101

volunteer work, 11

W–Z

Watch Repairers, 114

Water and Liquid Waste Treatment Plant and System Operators, 75

Water Transportation Occupations, 124

Weighers, Measurers, Checkers, and Samplers, Recordkeeping, 89–90

Welding, Soldering, and Brazing Workers, 115

Woodworkers, 114

work environment, 10, 66–68

work experience, 50–51

workplace readiness, 18

worksheets

Adaptive Skills Checklist, 19–21

Career Clues, 51

Career Interest Areas Checklist, 44–50

Career Planning Clues, 52

Characteristics of the People I Would Prefer to Work With, 69

Education and Training, 26–29

The Job and Volunteer History, 30–38

Job Exploration Worksheet, 169–171

My Acceptable Pay Range, 62

My Ideal Career, 150–152

My Job Objective, 164–165

My Most Important Values, 58–59

My Preferred Level of Responsibility, 63

My Preferred Work Environment, 67–68

My Top Job Titles, 125

Other Life Experiences, 39–41

Overnight Career Choice Matrix, 154–156

Preferred Geographic Location, 65

Special Knowledge or Interests I Might Use in My Next Job, 66

The Three Most Important Things to Include in My Ideal Career, 152

Transferable Skills Checklist, 22–24

What Makes You a Good Worker?, 19

Work Values Checklist, 55–58

writing skills, 143